music works

Kathie Barrs

Line drawings by Kathie Barrs

First published in 1994 by
BELAIR PUBLICATIONS LIMITED
P.O. Box 12, Twickenham, England, TWI 2QL
© 1994 Kathie Barrs

Series Editor Robyn Gordon
Designed by Richard Souper
Photography by Kelvin Freeman
Typesetting by Belair
Printed and Bound in Hong Kong by World Print Ltd
ISBN 0 947882 28 6

Acknowledgements

The Author and the Publishers would like to thank the following, for their invaluable help and support during the preparation of this book:

- Sally Melling, the staff and the children of Westfields Primary School, London, SW13

- Dawn Dobb for the Indonesian Dance artwork on page 65

- The children of Great Bardfield School, Braintree, Essex

- Katie Gordon for the cover artwork

- Robina Beckles Willson for her musical expertise.

Contents

Introduction

The main prerequisites for teaching music to young children are enthusiasm, a sense of rhythm and pitch, an ability to sing a tune, a willingness to learn and not to be afraid of making mistakes - and a belief that music is important.

You do not have to play an instrument to teach music - there are many more exciting and successful ways to help children to enjoy it. Music-making involves singing, dancing, composing, playing, moving, creating, and listening. Playing the piano can be an excellent tool, but it can also be a barrier between you and the children, and it is often better to sing with them, rather than play, as they learn through imitation.

Music is a natural part of each individual. Few children can sit still when listening to a piece of dance music, or fail to respond to the rhythm felt in a piece of poetry, while playgrounds echo to the sound of skipping rhymes.

Music education involves the whole child, using melody, rhythm, speech and movement. It has close links with other subjects, and provides a foundation for achievement in other areas of the curriculum through the development of auditory awareness and discrimination, improved motor skills, experience of collaborative learning situations, fluency in speech and, hopefully, improved self confidence and a sense of imagination. Creative work in music develops the skills of decision making and selection; and sharing in the creative processes of their friends can teach children sensitivity and respect.

Children live in a noisy world, where they need to learn how to listen and how to understand. They are always hearing, but there is not much chance for reflection and assimilation. Music education can help with this, allowing them opportunities to build their own images in their heads in response to songs, or to music they have heard or composed themselves.

Most importantly, if you enjoy it, they will too!

Kathie Barrs

Instruments

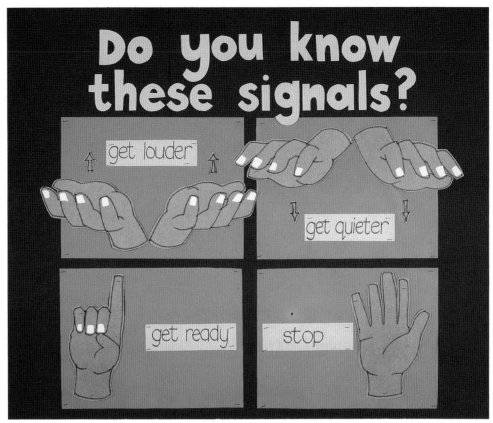

Simple hand signs to lead music-making sessions

The most common types of musical instruments used in the classroom are percussion instruments. These are instruments that have a resonating surface, which is struck with another object to make a sound, e.g. a drumstick.

Percussion instruments can be untuned, such as a tambourine or triangle, where the note that is made cannot be made to go higher or lower.

Alternatively, percussion instruments can be tuned, such as glockenspiels, metallophones, xylophones or chime bars.

GLOCKENSPIELS have a small wooden box with metal bars, and can be Alto or Soprano.
METALLOPHONES are larger, have aluminium bars and can be Alto, Soprano or Bass.
XYLOPHONES have wooden or fibreglass bars and can be Alto, Soprano or Bass.
CHIME BARS are a cheaper alternative. They are individual metal bars supported over a sound box. It is probably best to buy the 13 bars from C to top A, together with F# and Bb.

The most popular classroom percussion instruments are listed below, in five categories:

Metal	Wood	Skin	Hollow	Tuned
Indian Bells	Claves	Tambour	Maracas	Glockenspiel
Triangle	2 tone Woodblock	Bongos	Cabasa	Xylophone
Woodblock	Woodblock	Conga	Shakers	Chime bars
Cymbals - pairs	Agogo	Bass drum	Guiro	Metallophone
- stand	Castanets	Timpani Drum		
Sleigh Bells		Side drum		
Jingle stick		Tambourine		
Tambourine				
Cowbells				

Care of Instruments

Instruments should be stored in an easily accessible place, usually on a mobile trolley which can be moved as required. They should not be near any source of heat or direct sunlight, and should be covered when not in use, to protect them from dust.

Tuneable percussion such as Tambours and Drums which have tuning screws at the sides should have their screws greased regularly with petroleum jelly, and the screws slackened off after use to prevent the skins splitting by contracting in dry conditions.

Whoever uses the instruments must have respect for them, and know how to care for them.

Introducing the Instruments

● Before you start any games, it is vital to establish ground rules, as with all other classroom activities. Don't be afraid to expect high standards of behaviour in music sessions, as this can prevent broken instruments, over-excitement and headaches!

● Go through a small selection of instruments at the beginning of each session, until the children are familiar with the playing methods of each. Discuss with them the way that each instrument makes its sound.

● To establish a method of working, before the instruments are distributed ask the children to help you make up a series of 'conducting' signals that can be used universally by the children and you. For example, raised hands mean 'Stop playing immediately!' (see photograph page 5).

● Once the children have either chosen or been given an instrument, they must keep it absolutely silent until it is their turn to play.

● When the children realise that everyone will have a turn eventually, there is no need for them to express impatience.

● It is usually a good idea to sit in a circle, often with the instruments in the centre.

● Either allow the children to choose their instruments a few at a time, distribute them yourself, or specify the type of instrument, e.g. metal, that each child should choose. Get this part over quickly to avoid restlessness.

PLAYING UNTUNED INSTRUMENTS

The playing methods for most instruments are self-evident, and the children should be taught the correct methods, as well as being encouraged to experiment with other ways of making sounds. Ask them to devise their own methods of playing, which may include some of the following:

Tambour   - Hold it vertically, and tap on the other hand, or on the hip.
                 - Sit and hold it between the knees, using two hands to play.
                 - Press the skin of the tambour with one hand, and play with the other.
                   This alters the pitch.
                 - Lay it on the floor and play with two hands.

Tambourine   - Turn it over and tap the rim to get a 'jingle' sound.
                 - Wet the thumb and skid it around the rim to vibrate the skin.

Cymbal   - Use two beaters in one hand, separated by the forefinger. Slide the edge
                   of the cymbal between them and 'wobble' the beaters rapidly to play a trill.
                 - Use two cymbals and rub the faces together in a circular motion.

Triangle   - Place the beater in the corner of the triangle, and make fast circular
                   movements to play a trill.

Water chimes used to introduce notation through colour

Cabasa	- Rest the beads on the palm of one hand and twist the handle with the other hand to make a crisp sound.
	- Tap the beads on the palm of the hand.
Claves	- Hold one clave horizontal on the palm of the hand, cupping the hand to make a sound box. Tap this clave with the other one.
Indian Bells	- Hold them by the string, close to the bells themselves. Lower one bell on top of the other.
	- Play them like a miniature pair of cymbals.

GAMES TO PLAY WITH UNTUNED INSTRUMENTS

The Chain Game

This game can be adapted to suit your requirements. The children sit in a circle, each with a percussion instrument. Give them a directive, such as 'Make one sound on your instrument. Do not play it until the sound of the instrument played before you has almost died away. Try not to leave a gap before you make your sound.' This takes great concentration to be done properly.

Some suggestions may be:

- As above, but try to make an unusual sound with your instrument - don't play it in the conventional way.

- If you have an instrument that makes a long sound, try to fool everyone by making a short sound on it, and vice versa.
- Put someone in the centre of the circle with a cymbal. They direct proceedings by playing on their instrument, and then pointing to someone else to play theirs before the cymbal sound dies away. The list of variations is endless!

Can you Join in?

In a circle, give out a limited range of types of instruments - perhaps five types. Get the children to close their eyes, and you play one of the chosen instruments. All those with matching instruments can join in. Have a sound to indicate 'Stop', and repeat with a different instrument.

How's it Made?

Investigate the different ways in which sounds are made on instruments, such as:
'Accidental' sounds made while doing something else, e.g. leg bells jingling when walking.
'Intentional' sounds made with two hands, e.g. a pair of cymbals.
'Hand' sounds, made by tapping an instrument with a hand, e.g. tambourine.
'Striking' sounds, made with a hand or beater/beaters, e.g. a drum. (See photograph page 59.)

Obstacle!

Set up a simple obstacle course to be negotiated by someone who is blindfolded. Pre-arrange with that child a set of signals played on instruments that will be given to guide them through the course, e.g. a note on the triangle means turn 90º to the left.

PLAYING TUNED INSTRUMENTS

● The timbre, or quality, of the noise made by a percussion instrument can be altered by using a variety of beaters. Using the correct beater for each instrument will produce the best all-round sound, but alternative beaters will give more interesting effects. Don't stay with conventional beaters; experiment with other materials, such as pencils, marbles rolled along the bars, wire brushes, ping pong balls bounced along the bars and metal rods (be careful not to damage the instrument). Try the ridged handles of the beaters, dragged across the end of a bar. Use the wooden sound box as a drum.
Remove one of the bars and use it as a beater - gently!

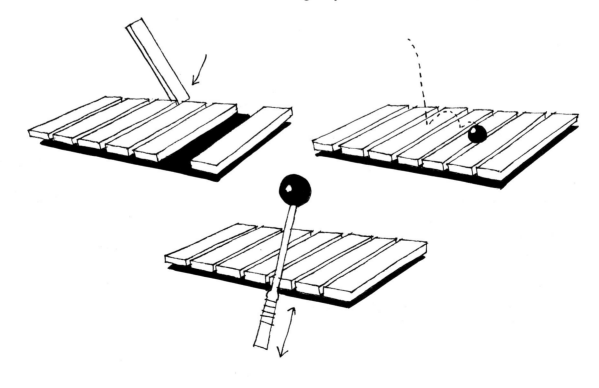

● It is important to teach the children to hold the beaters correctly. They should always play with a beater held loosely in each hand, and should practise alternating hands as they play. To get a good sound quality, the beaters should 'bounce' off the bars; tell the children to pretend that the bars are hot and they must not burn their beaters! The head of the beater should strike the bars in the centre. Do check that the rubber strips on which the bars rest are in good order, otherwise the vibrations will be deadened. The bars are arranged with the longest to the left. It is a good exercise for the children to remove all the bars - use two hands to do this so that the pins holding the bars are not bent - and replace them in the correct order.

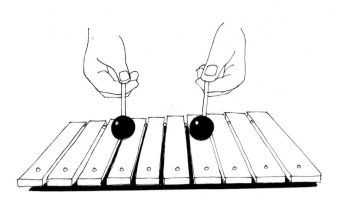

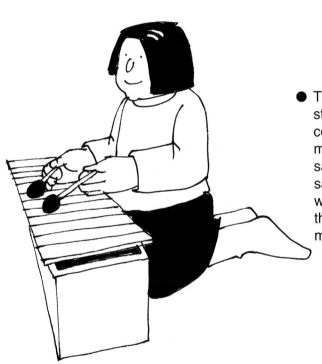

● The children can play the instruments kneeling, standing or sitting. It should be at a height that is comfortable and allows for free, relaxed arm movements. If two players are working on the same instrument, they should be positioned on the same side. When the children are beginning to work with tuned instruments, remove all the bars except the ones needed for that session. As they become more accurate, the other bars can be replaced.

● Investigate different ways of playing the tuned instruments. Try a glissando, when the beater is rested on the bars and drawn up and down them quickly. Or a tremolo, when two beaters are held in one hand, separated by the index finger. One beater is placed above the bar and the other below. The beaters are then wobbled to strike the bar alternately. Chords (more than one note playing at one time) can be played with two beaters in one hand, separated by the index finger to the correct distance, or with a beater in each hand.

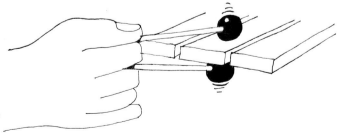

GAMES TO PLAY WITH TUNED INSTRUMENTS

● Group the children, according to how many instruments are available, so that there are perhaps four children to each metallophone. Establish a playing order, perhaps by numbering the children. Don't necessarily choose them to play in numerical order, so that they never know whose turn it will be next.

● To make playing easier, remove all but three of the bars, either C, E and G - or F, A and C. Ask the children to take turns to play a walking tune, using the beaters in both hands.

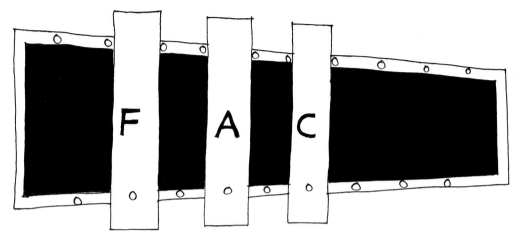

● Position the groups so that they cannot see each other's instruments. Ask group one to play a walking tune consisting of three notes, for example, G C E. Then ask the other groups to copy it, one at a time.

● Allow each group a turn to make up a tune, increasing the number of notes they have to work with as they become more accurate. The other groups try to echo these tunes. The children could go on to record their tunes, either on a tape-recorder or on paper.

● As their skill develops, extend this to playing a skipping tune or another kind of rhythm, and ask them to devise a way of recording either their own tune, or that of another group.

● Replace all bars on the instruments. As before, the game is to echo tunes created by another group.

● The children play up the scale, i.e. strike each bar consecutively, starting at the bottom. They then immediately choose one of the notes to play again once. The next group repeats the activity and sees if they can judge which was the last note. This encourages them to listen to intervals, which are the distances between notes.

USING THE INSTRUMENTS AS ACCOMPANIMENTS

● Choose a well-known song and allow half the class to sing, while the rest accompany on their instruments. Then swap over.

● Repeat this activity, with you conducting the playing (see photograph page 5). Introduce signs for loud/soft, getting faster/getting slower (see photograph on page 5).

● Talk to the children about the dangers of drowning songs with loud instruments, and ask for suggestions about ways to deal with this.

● Group the instruments according to various criteria, e.g. method of playing, materials from which they are made, etc. Allow specific groups to accompany songs.

● Get the children to conduct.

● The children who are not playing enjoy accompanying on 'pretend' instruments.

● Try different instruments on different verses. Discuss the use of instruments to create a mood or match a subject, e.g. woodblocks for a song about a clock.

Keep these early sessions short, regular and relaxed. You will find that some children play the beat, and others play the rhythm of the words. Don't worry at this stage about 'correcting' this, as it is one of the skills that they will be learning.

The Music Area

It is sometimes not easy to set up a music area in every classrom, but it is often possible to have one for a short time, maybe in an area outside the room, but near enough to be under the control of the teacher. As with all musical activities, the children need to know what is acceptable behaviour, and be responsible for the maintenance and care of the instruments in that area.

The music area allows everyone to work at their own pace, and to reinforce skills introduced by the teacher.

Limiting the number and range of instruments available at one time leads to more careful decision-making by the children, and encourages them to listen to and consider the sounds they are making.

Change the selection of instruments regularly, and withdraw the music area for a time when you feel that it is either being misused, or the children are becoming bored with it.

USING THE MUSIC AREA TO BEST ADVANTAGE

● Put out a selection of home-made shakers to play various games:
  - Make two of each type, e.g. two containing raisins, two containing rice, etc. Ask the children to match up the pairs.
  - Provide a selection of labels naming the contents, and ask the children to label the containers according to their contents.
  - Ask them to sort the containers according to various criteria, e.g. those with soft contents, those with one item inside, etc.

● Using a range of percussion instruments, get the children to put them in order of volume (loudest first), pitch (lowest first), or length of sound (longest first).

● Put out the chime bars, and let the children arrange them in order. Repeat the same activity with a glockenspiel, removing the bars and asking the children to reassemble.

● Make wind, water or flower pot chimes. Get the children to order them, label them in some way, and write tunes for them. (See photograph on page 7.)

● Devise some way of preventing two children from seeing each other's actions, e.g. a screen or large cardboard box. Place an identical selection of instruments on each side of the screen. The children take it in turns to play one of the instruments, and their partner attempts to match the sound.

● The children can devise their own sound effects for Nursery Rhymes or well-known poems, or write an accompaniment to their own stories and poems.

● When using tuned instruments in the Music Area, simple cards can be introduced, giving the notes for parts of well-known songs. For example, for Three Blind Mice, you could have the chime bars E, D and C put out, with the relevant card.

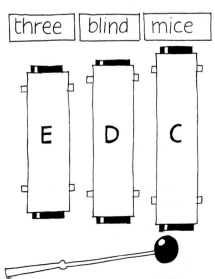

- A tape recorder gives the children the opportunity to listen to pre-recorded music for inspiration, and to record their own music-making sessions. Recorded radio programmes can also be available for listening to.

- If the noise is too much, consider 'Quiet Music Making' sessions, when the instruments provided all lend themselves to making quiet sounds! Use items such as shakers filled with sand or rice, triangles, sandpaper blocks and very fluffy beaters.

- Link the Music Area to topic work, and other activities in the classroom.

- Take an interest in the children's achievements. As with other areas of the curriculum, the children will produce better work when it is valued and shared by others. Occasionally, encourage them to work on a 'performance' piece, to be played to the rest of the class, which will in turn inspire others.

- Having a selection of stimuli, such as evocative photographs, poems, drawings, books, puppets etc. can inspire imaginative results.

- Set up a table in the classroom and have a changing display of 'sound makers'. Challenge the children to find many different ways of making sounds using the materials you have set out.

  - Provide a set of objects in a particular material, e.g. metal. Don't just use conventional instruments, such as triangles, jingle bells, glockenspiels, jingle sticks, cabasas. Include such things as an egg whisk, milk bottle tops, a screwdriver, etc.
  - Put one interesting item on the table with a large range of beaters. An old-fashioned metal kettle or watering can would be a good example.
  - Use a range of different containers, and put the same item in each. Get the children to investigate the various sounds that are made by the same object.
  - Reverse the above idea, so that you use several identical containers, and place different items inside them. You may want to have a theme, e.g. fruit and nuts.

- To inspire the children, supply suggestions and challenges written on cards. For example, 'Can you make a long sound?' 'What do you think is inside the yoghurt pot?' 'What happens when you put a ping pong ball inside the kettle and shake it?'

Rhythm and Beat

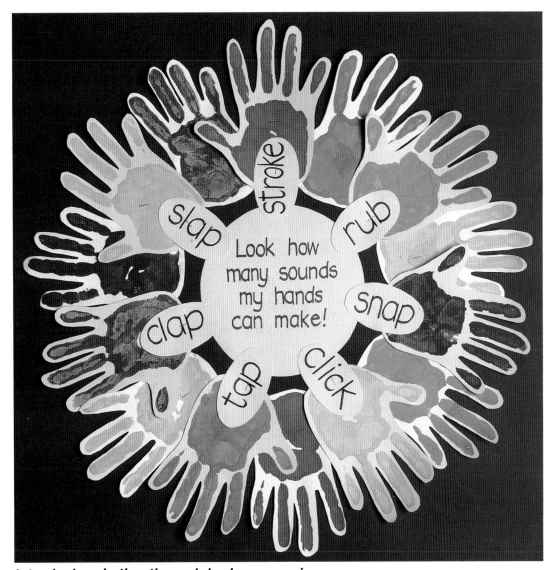

Introducing rhythm through body percussion

A sense of rhythm is very natural to us. From a very early stage in our lives, we are exposed to the sound of our mother's heartbeat, and as children are soothed by a rhythmic rocking motion. Being held and rocked, even as an adult, is very comforting. Some children may not have been made aware of this natural sense, and will therefore need more sensory experiences and practice in order to tune into it.

Beat is the regular pulse running through a piece of music. It is the one that makes you want to tap your foot, or clap your hands. Music with a strong beat is often dance music or marching music, for obvious reasons.

Rhythm is that aspect of music which relates to timing, and is a sequence of sounds of differing lengths. Ask the children to clap the rhythm of a well known rhyme (i.e. the pattern of the words) and point out that some of the notes are long and the others short. This pattern is the rhythm.

Allow plenty of relaxed and regular practice in tapping the pulse. Sometimes, ask the children to start the pulse by, for example, tapping their knees. Take the pulse from them and continue it on a drum, to allow them to feel a sense of satisfaction, and to experience the sensation of holding a beat.

RHYTHM GAMES

Rhythm games are some of the most enjoyable activities in the music curriculum. The list of ideas is endless, and can be added to constantly.

● The best way to start when introducing rhythm patterns, is with body percussion, i.e. making sounds with our own bodies. With the children in a circle, see how many different sounds they can make using only their hands (see photograph on page 13). How many times can you go around the circle with everyone having a new suggestion? (Encourage them to vary volume if they cannot find a new method, i.e. repeat someone else's idea, only louder.)

Clapping
hands cupped
hands flat
fingers only
fingers on palm
hands on knees - alternating left/right
                  alternating knees/hand clap

Try hands on the floor:

Tapping	fingertips fingernails knuckles whole fingers whole hand
Rubbing	as above
Slapping	as above
Cupping	as above
Banging	with fists etc.

Rubbing
hands together in a circular motion
in a cupped position
the backs of the hands together
fingers together

Tapping
knuckles
finger nails
finger tips

Snapping
fingers

Flicking
in the air
on the other palm

● In a circle, talk about different ways of moving around the room, e.g. running, skipping, limping, striding. Choose a child to demonstrate. You copy their rhythm on claves (or an equivalent). The children accompany by clapping.

● Now go on to use these 'hand percussion' sounds to accompany well known songs. Start with easy examples such as clapping or knee slaps.

    *   *   *   *
Baa baa black sheep

  *   *   *   *   *
Have you a-ny wool?

     *   *   *   *
Yes sir, yes sir,

     *   *   *
Three bags full.

Finding rhythm in familiar words

● Use every opportunity that arises to get the children to beat/clap/tap/stamp the pulse of a piece of music. The theme music of a television show, music played when they go into assembly, pre-recorded music, etc. all provide the chance for clapping along. They can clap their hands, their heads, the floor, their friends' hands - whatever they think of, as long as they are 'feeling' the beat as a physical experience. (When 'clap' is used in this section, any way of sounding a rhythm or pulse can be used, such as clicking, slapping, stamping, etc.)

● Ask the children to clap their names (echoing you first), or names of foods, animals, football teams, teachers. Be careful not to encourage exaggeration of the syllables. Say the names naturally without drawing them out (see photograph above).

● Play games where the children try to guess which name is being clapped, for example, when the children are lining up.

● Say a name and ask the children to clap it back to you.

● Organise two groups, each with a leader. Ask each to devise a very simple rhythm pattern, for example:

Count	1	2	3	4
Group 1	clap	knees	clap, clap	clap
Group 2	snap	clap, clap	clap	snap

Ask each group to perform, and then try them together. Get the leaders to use hand signals to start and stop their groups as they wish. They may need a steady drum beat to keep them together.

- Give out cards with either pictures or words on them, perhaps to do with a current topic. Beat a rhythm, e.g. dough-nut (two beats), and all those with a card matching that rhythm can stand up.

- Using cards again, divide the class into three groups. Each group is named after an animal - all with clearly differing rhythms to their names, e.g. gi-raffe, cat and ta-ran-tu-la. Each group takes a turn to say/clap/tap/click and play its rhythm. Build it into a 'performance', getting each group to follow on after the other. Investigate trying this as a round. Vary with volume and speed - get them to try whispering. Use a steady drum beat to keep them all together.

- Clap the rhythm of a well known nursery rhyme and ask the children to guess it.

- Clap the first line of a nursery rhyme, and get to the children to echo it. Go through the whole rhyme like this.

- Clap a rhythm, let the children echo it straight back to you. Immediately, clap another: they echo, you clap, they echo, etc. The aim is not to leave any space between your clap and their echo. To keep yourself going, think of the rhythm of words as a stimulus for each clap (for example, ma-ca-ro-ni cheese, ba-con and eggs, etc.).

- Put the children into groups. Each group chooses a different way to sound out a pulse. Either you or a child acts as a conductor, and when a group is pointed to, they beat/clap/click/stamp etc. the pulse. You could keep the beat regular by tapping a drum. Try two groups at once.

- Sing a song that the children know very well. Ask for suggestions for 'Body Percussion Accompaniment'. Try a few and ask the children to choose their favourite. For example:

clap	clap	click	click	clap	clap	click	click
Old	**Mac -**	**don -**	**ald**	**had**	**a**	**farm**	

clap	clap	click	click	clap	clap	click	click
Eee	**i**	**eee**	**i**	**Oh**		**...And**...etc.	

Allow the children plenty of practice to establish the pattern of clapping and clicking before attempting to do it with the song. Get half the group to sing, and the other half to sound the beat. Change over. Then do it with everyone singing and sounding the beat.
Make sure the beat is constant, even when there is no singing, such as at the end of the second line of 'Old Macdonald'.

- Practise clapping the first line of a song or nursery rhyme. Split the group into two. Clap the rhythm as a round, with one group starting and the other joining in at the appropriate place, e.g.

Group 1   **Baa baa black sheep, have you any wool?**
          * * *   *   * * ** *

Group 2   **Baa baa black sheep, have you any wool?**
                          * *   *   *   * ** *

- Vary this activity by going twice through the round, getting gradually louder, and then twice through again, getting gradually quieter.

- Try it as a three part round.

- Divide the group into two. Set up Group 1 clapping a walking beat and saying quietly 'walk, walk, walk'. Get Group 2 to clap a running beat, i.e. twice as fast, saying 'runn-ing, runn-ing, runn-ing'. To keep the speed constant, accompany them on a drum, playing a steady pulse with the 'walk' group.

- Sit in the centre of the circle with an instrument which plays a short, crisp note, e.g. claves or woodblock. Turn to each child individually, and play a short rhythm. Ask them to echo it in whatever way they choose.

- **Fade Out.**
  Choose a piece of catchy music with a heavy beat. Play it to the children, and ask them to devise a way of sounding the beat. This can be done with instruments or body percussion. Once everyone has established the beat, slowly turn down the volume, letting them continue playing for a short time. Bring back the music and see who is still in time!

- **Who is it?**
  Choose a topic, e.g. animals, and have pictures of four different animals. The children first say the names, and then clap them. When they are confident with this, allow them to devise games, e.g. one child claps the name of an animal and the rest have to identify it. Extend this by introducing percussion instruments on which to play the rhythms, and then tuned instruments on which the children can make up tunes for each animal name.

- **Mix up**.
  Divide the group into two. Using a topic, each group devises a sequence which they can clap and say, for example,

steady drum beat on pulse	#		#			#		#	
	*	*	*	*	*	*	*	*	
Group I	Don	- key	An-tel-ope			Ze-bra		Rat	
	*	*	*	*	*	*	*	*	*
Group 2	Chim-pan-zee		Ost - rich			Bat		Wil-de-beest	

- Invent various combinations, for example having one group chant their sequence whilst the other group claps theirs.

- **Take over.**
  Sit in a well spaced out circle. One child has an instrument and plays a rhythm on it, then walks around inside the circle, playing the rhythm until choosing someone to come and take over the instrument, by going to stand in front of that person. That chosen person then takes the instrument and repeats the rhythm, moving around to choose a new person while the original player sits in the vacated place. Once the children have mastered this, introduce another instrument at the same time, so that there are two rhythms being played simultaneously.

Notation

Before they come to consider writing music down, children need to have experienced a wide range of musical activities such as playing, dancing, clapping, singing, etc. which will have provided them with a strong sense of rhythm, pulse and pitch.

Discuss the ways in which ideas can be conveyed to others: by writing, by speaking, via television, etc. Ask the children to consider ways in which music can be written down so that others may come and share it. It is great fun, and need not take any musical skill or knowledge.

Show a selection of cards with abstract images on them. Discuss the sounds suggested by the symbols. Ask the children to make the sounds first with their mouths, and then with instruments.

GRAPHIC NOTATION
● The early stages of notation can simply be drawings done by the children to portray sounds they make or hear. Go on a Sound Walk, listening for noises inside and outside the school building (see photograph in Listening Skills chapter, page 49). This visual representation of sound is known as graphic notation. Children take to this form of written music very easily and are full of ideas for ways to show how to play their tunes.

● When introducing graphic notation, it is helpful to have whole group sessions, perhaps with access to a blackboard, when everyone can offer ideas. For example, ask the children for suggestions as to how to represent the concept of getting louder or softer, or the length of time a note should last, or how many times it should be played. The children will probably find it fascinating that different people come up with the same ideas, e.g. the duration of a note can be shown by the length of the stroke, and volume by the heaviness of the stroke.

● Give each child a large piece of paper and drawing implements suitable for large sweeping movements. Ask them to listen carefully to the sounds they can hear and to make marks on the paper to show those sounds. Go through these 'drawings' together, noting any similarities or differences in the way each sound was represented by the listener. Discuss.

Mouth Music
Investigate how many sounds the children can make with their mouths. Go round a circle with everyone contributing a different sound. Challenge them to write a piece of 'mouth music' and score it. Remind them about pitch (as the voice is a tuned instrument) as well as volume and duration.

Colour Scores
Make a water xylophone. Colour the water in each bottle with a different shade of food colouring. Get the children to compose music and work out tunes on it, and challenge them to notate their music so that others can come along and play it (see photograph in Instruments chapter, page 7).

Picture Scores. Allow the children to select a group of instruments each, and get them to draw and number each one. They can then record in which order they should be played, in which style, and how many times

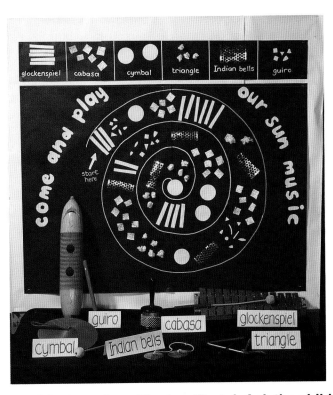

Junk Scores. Choose a subject, such as 'Sun' or 'Party'. Ask the children to select a range of instruments they see as suitable for describing this. Using 'recyclable materials' and a variety of papers, allocate a material to each instrument and create a 'score'

Poem Scores

Provide copies of evocative poems, and ask the children to write tunes to accompany them on tuned instruments set up for a pentatonic scale (e.g. CDEGA). They could write their score on the poem.

Group Tunes

● Ask the children to form groups, and create a body percussion sequence between them. Ask them to notate it. How can they convey speed and volume? Do they need a conductor to keep them together?

● As a pattern emerges in the children's work, it is possible to draw up a 'Class Notation Chart' with universally accepted symbols for use by everyone when composing.

● Make up a series of cards showing different arrangements of long and short sounds. Give the cards out and ask the children to create a sequence with either instruments or body percussion, based on their cards. For example, a card reading _____ _____   __ _____ __ __ __ could be interpreted as

＿＿＿ ＿＿＿ ＿ ＿＿＿ ＿ ＿ ＿
cymbal cymbal clap   cymbal   clap clap clap

● To instill a sense of timing, ask the children to fit their sequences into the time taken for someone else to play 10 drum beats. Can they incorporate that in their score? For example,

＿＿ ＿＿ ＿ ＿ ＿ ＿
1   2   3   4   5   6   7   8   9   10

Playing in Ensembles

The children will find that writing music for one person to play is quite different from writing music for an ensemble. They now need to take into account how to convey when each instrument begins to play, and when it stops.

Ask them to consider how to ensure that all those involved play at the same speed and come in at the right time. Do they need a conductor? Would it help to have one large copy of the score for all of them to follow? Could they use a system of bar lines, and have someone counting as they play?

Rests

A rest, in musical terms, is when nothing is happening.

● Make a series of cards, some with instruments being played and others with them not being played. Hold them up, one at a time, and ask the children to read the cards and make appropriate sounds and actions for a 'playing' card, and remain silent for a 'not playing' card. Try this with clapping, and with instruments.

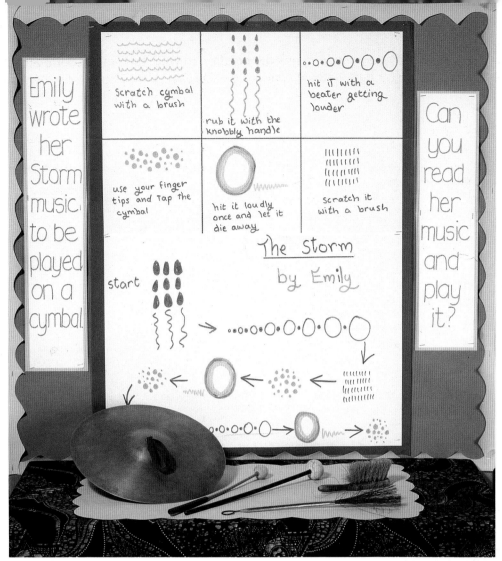

Score for One. Using only one instrument, ask the children how many sounds they can make on it, without causing damage! Get them to write down their ideas graphically, and then create a piece of music for others to play . They will probably need to devise a key to explain the symbols

● Make more complex versions, where rests and notes are mixed up together. Ask the children to write their own cards. Make sure that the children give the full value to rest beats, and do not skip over them. Do this by getting them to demonstrate the rest beats when they play. (If they are drumming, they could play the rest beat in the air beside the drum. If clapping, get them to hold their hands out, palms upwards.)

● Use four finger or ordinary puppets, each representing one beat. Give one to each of four children, and ask them to stand in a line, numbering themselves l, 2, 3 and 4. Ask them to either hold their puppet up, or down. The rest of the group count aloud to 4, clapping on the beats where the puppet is held up, and showing a rest when the puppet is down. The children can also play and write down these rhythms as shown by the puppets.

● Make cards based on the puppet idea, using a dotted outline to represent a rest.

● Show the children the standard sign for a one beat rest.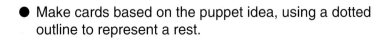

Picture the Beat

● Learn a song with a visual image, e.g. 'How much is that Doggie in the Window?' Allow the children to sing it, clap the beat, play it, march to it. If necessary, watch for someone who has the right beat and get the others to follow. Do it as a conga, all singing at the same time. Get half the group to sing and the other half to clap the beat.

● Have a set of prepared cards ready to go with the song - in this case, for example, illustrated with dogs. Get half the children to chant 'dog...dog...dog' on the beat, while the rest sing the song. Point to (or hold up) the pictures in time to the beat.

● Extend this by adding instruments as well. Try it in four groups, with each doing something different, perhaps all coming in one after the other.

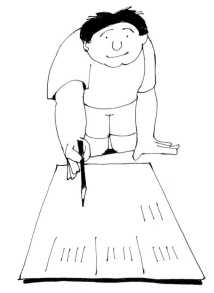

RHYTHMIC NOTATION

● Get half the class, or group, to sing a song such as 'Frère Jacques'. Ask the other half to write down the rhythm of the song. Look at the results together and discuss. You will probably find that most children have used a form of linear representation of the rhythm, with lines all over the page. Talk to them about sorting this out so that people can read it - books have words written in lines going one way, and music is similar. Suggest to them, if no one else suggests it, that the short notes sound as if they are running. They would like 'to run with a friend, so let them join hands'.

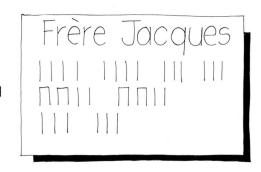

Rhythm Sticks

As a group, write the rhythm of 'Frère Jacques' together, using short and long notes. Call this method of notation 'rhythm sticks'. Clap the rhythm as it is written in order to check it.

Rhythm Cards

Make a series of cards with rhythms written using the rhythm stick method. Get the children to play/sing/clap/tap/walk them, and write their own.
Ask them to write their names using rhythm sticks.

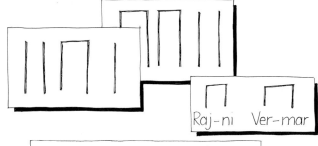

Large or Small

Using the idea of pictures again, small images can be used to represent short notes, and large images can be used for long notes. Get the children to write rhythms using pictures.

Improvisation

Using instruments for sound effects in stories

When children are involved in dramatic play, they automatically use sound effects, and will find, in most cases, that the step to improvising and creative music-making is a simple one. Initial attempts may be rather limited and unstructured, but if they are given plenty of opportunities to listen to, experience and discuss music, their own creative efforts will show a greater degree of discrimination and progression. Children will eventually find out by experimentation, but controlled exploration guided by the teacher is quicker.

In order to make the first few sessions of creative improvisation a success, keep everything very simple, and make the sessions fairly short. The children will really enjoy it, and even more so if they are clear what they are being asked to do. Children benefit from being encouraged to work in a structured environment when improvising. Activities need to be clearly directed, and the aims of the activity also understood by the participants. Most children initially find it difficult to work in a nebulous, free-for-all situation, preferring to have guidance, and their creativity will arise from increased knowledge and understanding of music.

Make clear to the children that you are expecting them to be able to perform their short composition to the rest of the group at the end of the session. This gives a purpose and a sense of urgency to the exercise, and adds to a feeling of achievement.

For creative music-making, as with writing, there is a need for a stimulus. Some ideas for stimuli are listed below:

weather, e.g. strong winds
events, e.g. a train journey
festivals, e.g. Chinese New Year
topic work, e.g. water
photographs
poems
stories
pictures and paintings

● Stories and poems can be written by the children for the purpose of music-making, and often the more simple ones are the most successful. A suggestion might be 'Our day out', and may lead to a story based on a trip to the park - skipping along the road (happy), running to the playground (fast), going on the swings (swinging music), the rain starting (little drops, getting faster and heavier, perhaps with thunder), running home (fast, panicky), getting home and the sun coming out again (happy).... (See photograph on page 23.)

ORGANISATION
● The circle is a safe and intimate environment in which to work, where all children can be seen and heard by the rest of the group. Already there should be well-established codes of practice when any type of music-making takes place, e.g. the children must not make a sound with their instruments until it is their turn.

24

● Have the instruments set out to enable the children to select easily and quickly.

● Use only one stimulus with the group for the first few sessions, and make sure that there is a lot of preliminary discussion of what kind of music they wish to make, and how they can achieve it. 'What would be a good instrument to make the sound of the first drops of rain falling?' Demonstrate this yourself, or ask a child to do it, and invite comments - 'Should the sound be louder/faster/crisper?' 'Could we get a better sound from a different instrument?' The more constructive the discussion, the more successful the session will be.

● Remind the children that no one wants to finish up with a headache, and that no instruments should get damaged. If you have already established a system of 'conducting signs' with your group, remind them of this, and say that you expect them to follow your signs. If this is a new concept for your group, introduce it now and devise a set of simple signs to communicate such vital messages as 'Everyone stop playing immediately!' or 'Keep the noise down!' (See photograph in Instrument chapter, page 5.)

● The children can be grouped according to several criteria, but it is often a good idea to ask the children individually, while they are still in the circle, which type of noise they would like to make, and then group them accordingly, i.e. one 'rain-maker', one 'swinger', one 'runner' etc. to each group. Do the grouping quickly after the discussions, so that the initial stimulus does not lose its power.

● Give the children a set period of time to produce an initial piece, and then let them go off to various corners of the room and start composing.
This part is a little noisy. Use your conductor signs if necessary. Keep the groups informed as to how their allocated time is progressing, e.g. 'Only two minutes to go', and when the time has elapsed, ask everyone to be quiet again, still sitting in their respective groups all over the room. Remind them of the need to share each other's compositions, whether in music or another curriculum area, and of the value of constructive criticism. Then go around the groups, asking for a performance - this is a kind of 'rough draft' which will be tidied up and perhaps changed around later.

● Everyone can offer suggestions and advice to the players. Some ideas may be:
  - The playing can be varied - with increases or decreases in volume and speed.
  - It is sometimes a good idea to include body percussion sounds in the piece, for example, fingers tapping on the floor for the first drops of rain.
  - The music could be arranged in several ways, for example:
      The instruments could be played one at a time.
      They could be played in larger groups.
      One instrument could be played all the way through, perhaps representing the child who is in the story from beginning to end.
      The instruments could come in one at a time, building up to a big finale.

  - Music needs a clear ending, so that the audience knows when to clap! If the piece is too short, suggest that they use a pattern of repeating sections,
      e.g. Beginning - A
            Middle - B
            End - C

They could plan an order such as A B A C.
Next, explain that they have perhaps five more minutes to polish up their composition before taking part in a finished 'production'.

Question and Answer
- Once the children are well practised in echoing, e.g. copying your clapping patterns, the concept of question and answer can be introduced. In this, rather than repeating a phrase, the second person makes up a different phrase which they consider follows the first one well. It sounds as if the first person has asked a question and the second person is answering it in their own way.

  The best way to introduce this is to do it through speech first. Ask each child the same question, e.g. 'What do you like to eat?' - and they reply accordingly.
  Now repeat this, but as well as asking the question, clap the rhythm at the same time. Get the children to reply by speaking and clapping as well. Now try it without the speech - just with the clapping patterns.

clap	clap	clap	clap	clap	clap		clap	clap	clap	clap	clap	clap
What	do	you	like	to	eat?		Spag -	he -	tti	bo -	log -	naise

- Extend this idea by combining different body sounds:

click	knees	knees	clap	clap	click		head	clap	clap	stamp	stamp	click
What	do	you	like	to	eat?		Spag -	he -	tti	bo -	log -	naise

- Try this with untuned percussion instruments. You ask the children a 'question' on a drum, and they reply on, for example, a woodblock.

- When the children are confident in clapping responses to your questions, sit in a circle. Firstly, clap the same 'question' to each child in turn around the circle, and let them clap an 'answer'. It does not matter if a child repeats someone else's answer. To help you to remember your 'question', keep a phrase in your head and use that for the rhythm, e.g.

  sailing on an ocean, bobbing up and down

  Try to 'keep the kettle boiling', without any hiccups!

- Then go around the circle in the same way again, but this time, instead of your repeating the same 'question' each time, clap a different one to each child. Just try to let your hands do the work - if you try to think about a rhythm, you may find that you seize up, and the whole point of doing this exercise is to keep the clapping continuous without hiccups.

- Next, clap a question to the first child in the circle. The child answers you, and then he/she turns and claps a question to the next child. Again, that child answers and then turns and claps a question to the next child, etc.

- The final version is very fast moving when it is done properly without any gaps in the rhythm. You clap a question, to child l. Child l replies and this reply serves as a question to child 2, who replies to it. This reply is also a question to child 4, and so on. Try and go around the circle without any hold ups!

SINGING IMPROVISATION GAMES

Simple games can be played with the children, using question and answer songs. Register is an ideal time, and although you may feel self-conscious at first, the children love this.

● Rather than saying the names, sing them on the two notes used when we call 'Coooo-eeee'. Ask the children to suggest ideas for their responses, using the same two notes:

Marion   **I'm here** or **Here today** or **Good morning all**

● Using the three notes call of 'I'm the king of the castle', play games such as
Who has buckles on their shoes?
We have buckles on our shoes.
You can go out to play then.
The range of games to be played using the three note call is endless, once the children have got used to the idea.

IMPROVISING WITH TUNED INSTRUMENTS

● Begin this work using the two notes E and G only. This is simple if the children are using chime bars, but if they are using glockenspiels, xylophones and metallophones, remove all the bars except E and G.

● Ask the children to play their names on the two notes. Play various games, such as asking them to play their friend's name, guessing who is playing which name, and so on.

● Go on to Question and Answer games as in the section above, where the children reply on instruments, to questions asked both by you and the other children.

● Gradually, over a series of sessions, extend the range of notes available to the children, in the following order: E G A D C
This is known as the pentatonic scale of C. A pentatonic scale is five notes selected from an octave (seven notes) and it allows any notes in a tune written using this scale to sound harmonious. When several tuned instruments are improvising together, providing that they are all set up to the same pentatonic scale, anything that is played on them will sound harmonious.

To set up an instrument in the pentatonic scale of C:

As you can see, the fourth and seventh notes in a scale are removed to make it pentatonic.

● Using the same rhythm cards used for clapping games (see page 22), ask the children to make up tunes for them using a tuned instrument set up with a pentatonic scale.

Standard Notation

Standard notation is the traditional way of writing down music. After the children have had experience of writing and reading graphic notation, discuss with them the need to have a set of symbols which everyone can understand, once they have learned the meanings of the symbols.

BAR LINES
In western notation, music is divided into 'bars' or sections. These sections are separated by vertical lines called bar lines and the music is written in between them. In music, there is a natural regular 'heavy' beat, and this heavy beat falls on the first note after the bar line. Make it clear to the children that you do not stop at a bar line.

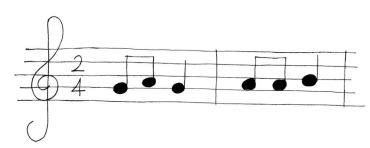

● Listen to a piece of music with a strong pulse that makes you want to tap your feet. You should find that every third or fourth beat (depending on whether the music is written with three or four beats to the bar) will feel stronger than the other beats. This is known as the 'accented beat' and is the first note in the bar.
Play this music to the children and get them first to clap the pulse or beat. Talk about the accented beat and encourage them to feel this. Then they could try slapping their knees on the accented beat and clapping to the other beats. Get them to walk to the beat, dipping one knee on the stressed beat.

● Repeat the above activity, chanting 'ONE' on the accented beat, and 'two, three' or 'two, three, four' for the other beats. Make the 'ONE' much louder than the other numbers.

● Ask half the group to sing a familiar song and the rest to clap or chant on the accented beat, for example:

Group 1	**zoo**	**zoo**
Group 2	**Daddy's taking us to the zoo tomorrow**	
Group 1	**zoo**	**zoo**	
Group 2	**Zoo tomorrow, zoo tomorrow**	
Group 1	**zoo**	**zoo**
Group 2	**Daddy's taking us to the zoo tomorrow**	
Group 1	**zoo**	**zoo**	
Group 2	**We can stay all day**	

● When this activity is fully understood, extend it by using three groups and adding instruments:
   Group 1 plays tambourines on every beat
   Group 2 plays triangles on the accented beat
   Group 3 sings the song

● Try this with a piece of recorded music replacing the song.

Using notes to represent the rhythm of names

● Play a steady beat on a drum, accenting every fourth beat. Divide the group into two sections. Group 1 make a sound on every beat, and group 2 make a sound only on the accented beat.

● Try this in three time (accented beat every three beats) or two time (accented beat every two beats).

● Listen to some music and ask the children to identify how many beats in the bar, i.e. if the accented beat is 'ONE', how many beats are there after it, before the next heavy beat?
  - 'ONE two ONE two' means there are two beats in the bar (two time).
  - 'ONE two three ONE two three' means there are three beats in the bar (three time).
  - 'ONE two three four ONE two three four' means there are four beats in the bar (four time).
  A march would probably be in two time.
  Waltz music is useful for this activity as it is strongly accented in three time.
  Rock and roll is usually written in four time.

● Ask the children to make groups of three, and number themselves I, 2 and 3
  - Child 1 quietly chants a related word on the beat.
  - Child 2 makes a related sound on the accented beat.
  - Child 3 chants a nursery rhyme.

For example:

Child 1	**lamb**	**lamb**	**lamb**	**lamb**	
Child 2	**Baa**		**Baa**		
Child 3	**Mary**	**had a**	**little**	**lamb**	

Child 1		**lamb**		**lamb**	**lamb**	**lamb**
Child 2		**Baa**			**Baa**	
Child 3	**It's**	**fleece was**		**white as snow**		

RHYTHM NOTATION

There are many systems available for the teaching of rhythm notation. Once the children are familiar with writing and reading Rhythm Sticks (see page 22) the transition to standard notation is relatively easy.

The key to rhythm notation is through syllables in words, and the children should have had plenty of practice in hearing and interpreting long and short syllables (see photograph page 15).

● Use percussion instruments to explain the different lengths of the musical notes. Play one note on each of the following instruments:

Woodblock	(the sound stops immediately - ask the children to imitate the sound with a single clap, while counting 'One')
Metallophone	(the sound continues longer - ask the children to imitate this sound, clapping on 'one' and then, with the hands clasped, raising them and lowering them on 'two'. Explain to them that this sound is twice as long as that of the woodblock)
Cymbal	(the sound is twice as long as that of the metallophone, so the children clap on the count of 'One' and then raise and lower their clasped hands three times while counting 'Two, Three, Four')

● Next, introduce the method of writing down these note values -
  - The woodblock is a 'quarter note' and is written ♩ (count 1)

  - The Metallophone represents a 'half note' and is written ♩ (count 2)

  - The cymbal is a 'whole note' and is written ○ (count 4)

● To the accompaniment of a steady drum beat, show the children notation cards for them to clap, counting aloud, and later in their heads.

● Invent names for the notes, the number of syllables relating to the number of beats each represents. For example,

stride   **walking**   **runn-ing quick-ly**   OR   **mum   da-ddy**   **li-ttle   chil-dren**

● Teach the children the names of the system you have decided to adopt, for example, Kodaly:-

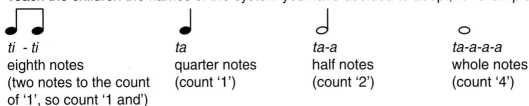

ti - ti	*ta*	*ta-a*	*ta-a-a-a*
eighth notes	quarter notes	half notes	whole notes
(two notes to the count of '1', so count '1 and')	(count '1')	(count '2')	(count '4')

Introduce the relationships of whole, half, quarter and eighth notes.

WRITING IT DOWN

● When the children have had plenty of practice with this idea and can work confidently, introduce the idea of applying it to instruments and writing it down. Start with the whole group together, using three instruments and a large chart which everyone can see. Remind the children of the standard notation for a rest and discuss when each instrument should play. Write the score together with the children on a large chart, one instrument at a time.

- Point out the bar lines which divide the music into sections. Explain that they are like fence posts, marking the music into sections, and that each section must have its full value of four beats, made up either of notes or rests. Remind the children that the first beat after the bar line is a heavy, accented beat, and that you don't stop at the bar lines!

- Practise playing this music. Then divide the class into groups of three and ask them to write their own music in this style. Come back together, ask them to perform their own music, and then get them to play that of another group. They may find that they need a conductor tapping out or counting aloud the steady beat to keep them together.

- Extend this by initially keeping the groups and instruments the same, and writing a different piece of music.

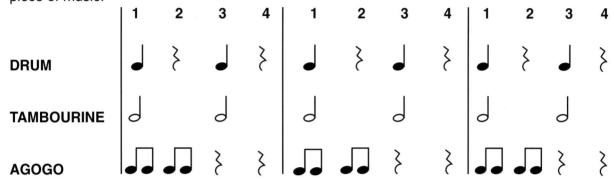

- Give the children lots of experience in writing rhythms to fit into a certain number of beats. Hold a competition to see who can come up with the most combinations of a rhythm in three beats. Remind them about using rests.

USING WORDS
- Extend previous work which will have been done on the children's names by relating this to notation. Ask half the group to whisper 'one...two...one...two' while the rest, in turn, say their name in the time it takes to say 'one...two' (remind them not to distort their names):

one two	one two	one and two
Tom	**Pan-nee**	**Je- ssi- ca**

- Now, with the children's help, produce name cards with the rhythmic notation for each name. Remember that each name is said to the count of two (see photograph on page 29).

- Extend this work by making rhythm notation cards for subjects other than names, e.g. items of clothing, animals, days of the week. Say the words to the count of two, as before:

- Reinforce this by playing games, for example: Using cards with only the notations written on them, match the right name to the right card. Put the rhythms to music and sing the names, performing the rhythms with body percussion, etc.

- Sit in a circle, and pass a drum around, chanting: 'Pass the drum around the ring. When it stops, play something!' The child holding the drum at the end of the verse plays one of three rhythms displayed somewhere in the room, and then chooses someone to identify which was played.

Melodic Notation

Written music needs to show both rhythm (the length of each note) and melody (the pitch of each note - whether it is higher or lower than the one before).

Work on melodic notation should not start until the children have experienced a rich variety of singing, playing and listening experiences, and have developed a sense of pitch.

PITCH

● Make up phrases about things going up and down, and use the pitch of the voice to show the up and down movements, e.g.
'Put your umbrella right up' (said with the voice going up)
'When the rain starts coming down' (said with the voice going down)

● Repeat this, introducing body movements to correspond with the change of pitch, e.g. hands going up and down.

● Play games in which the children move around the room in a high or low fashion, according to the music they hear, which could be recorded music, or a tune played by the teacher. Discuss which animals we connect with low notes (elephants, bears, etc.) and which with high notes (birds, butterflies, etc.). Ask the children to move in the style of one of these animals in response to a musical stimulus.

● Play a high note on a piano, and ask the children to move towards you. Then play a low note, and ask them to move away from you. Alternate low and high notes to control the children's movements.

● Hide two chime bars, one high and one low. One child plays one of them, and the others guess whether it is the high one or the low one. The person who guesses correctly has the next turn to play. Progress to playing two notes, one note on each of the chime bars, and the audience has to say whether the order of playing was 'high then low' or 'low then high'.

● Use finger puppets. Start with two and hold one high and one low. Play games such as getting the children to make the puppet talk in a high voice, etc. Develop this into singing games where some children hold the finger puppets at different heights and the rest hum the tune shown by them. Increase the number of puppets. Ask the children to arrange them to show the tune of the first line of a well known song.

Hot   cross   buns

● Play games with tuned instruments, such as musical 'Hunt the Thimble'. Hide an object in the classroom, and ask a child to hunt for it. Rather than giving verbal clues such as 'You're getting warmer!', give musical clues such as playing higher notes as the child moves towards the object, and lower ones when he moves away.

Eight Giraffe Babies Dance Fast

Mnemomics used to remember the notes of the stave

● Use tuned instruments to play music for a rocket blasting off, or Jack and Jill falling down the hill, or someone falling out of a tree, etc. Make cards to represent the music going up and down and ask the children to select the correct card to match the music. Use these cards to play games, as follows:

● Play five notes going up and ask a child to choose the matching card. Repeat for card 2 and card 3. Play two cards one after the other, and ask which they were.

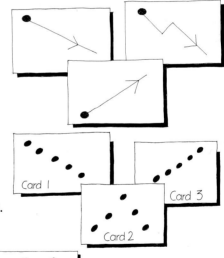

● Repeat, playing a combination of all the cards, and ask a child to put them in the correct order. Progress to cards with more complex tunes.

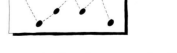

● Sing nursery rhymes with simple two or three note melodies, for example, 'See Saw Marjory Daw'. Ask the children to show the music with their hands by holding one hand horizontally in the air at chest height as they sing, and moving it up and down as the melody goes up and down.

● Now provide the children with a paper with the chime bars drawn on it and ask them to write their music on this.

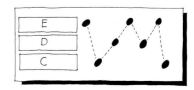

INTRODUCING NAMES OF NOTES

Set out F and G chime bars and ask the children to create a piece of music on themand then write it down. They will probably record it using the letter names, e.g.

F G F F F G G F G

Ask them then to show the pattern of the music visually as well, below the letters:

```
F  G  F  F  F  G  G  F  G
   *           *  *     *
*     *  *        *
```

● Now provide the children with a paper with the chime bars drawn on it and a line drawn next to G. Ask them to write their music on this.

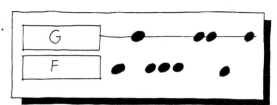

● Add chime bar A. The children can then write music for these three bars.

● Now put out chime bars G and B. Ask the children to compose a tune on these two bars. Consider writing down this tune. Draw chime bar G and a line as before. What note is below the line? (F) What note is above the line? (A). So, where can we write the notes to be played on chime bar B? Someone will suggest drawing in another line for B.

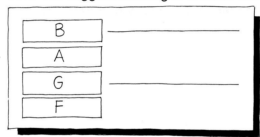

This exercise stresses the importance of the spaces between the lines - they represent places where the notes can be written, as well as on the lines.

MAGNET BOARD

● Use a magnet board or a large tin tray, and a selection of animal fridge magnets. Attach paper on the board to represent the sky and the ground. Arrange the magnets on the board, some on the ground and some in the air, to represent a melody line (see photograph on following page). Play the melody on a tuned instrument, the high notes being A and the low notes being F, as in the tune of the first line of 'See Saw Marjory Daw'. The magnets in the air are high notes (A), and the ones on the ground are lower notes (F). Get the children to hum or 'la' the melody you have written. Ask the children to make up their own melodies.

● When this concept of high and low is established, replace the horizon with a line. Place some of the magnets above the line (high note, for example, A), and others below the line (low note, for example F). Sing the melody.

● Next, introduce a third note (G) which is represented by a magnet figure sitting on the line. Make up tunes with the figures, and play and sing them.

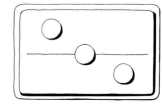

34

Move our monsters to make a new tune.

Magnet figures showing differences in pitch (see facing page)

● The idea can be transferred to paper, with the children drawing their own figures on, above and below a line on a piece of paper.

Notation
● Start by singing a two note 'call and response' game, using your hand to show the pitch of each note:

```
        *                *    *
              *                  *
  'Where's Jane?'      'Here  I  am.'
```

● Using the magnet board again, draw two lines across it, and put two magnet figures on the lines, the first on the top line and the second on the lower line, to represent the call, 'Where's Jane?' Get the children to sing as you point to the figures. Talk about the first note being higher than the second, etc.

● Then ask a child to show the response 'Here I am' using the magnet figures.

● Prepare a xylophone by removing all the bars except G and B. Lay the magnet board next to the xylophone so that the two lines correspond to the bars to let the children see that to play the response 'Here I am', they would play two notes on G, and one on B.

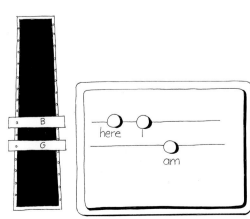

- The children can now use two lines drawn on a piece of paper to write their own two note melodies, using gummed paper circles, and play them on the xylophone. This is the beginning of using the full five line stave.

- Extend this activity by introducing the bar A on the xylophone (between G and B) and asking the children where they could write the note for A. Explain that there is no need to draw more lines, as there is a space in between the two already drawn. Ask the children to write three note melodies on G, A and B, and to play them.

- Now add chime bar C, and show the children where to write the note C on their paper. Introduce the other notes, one at a time, giving plenty of time for the children to practise writing and reading the notes as they learn them. Eventually, they will be working with a five line stave. Explain that Middle C has its own line below the stave to make it easy to recognise.

- Teach the children the mnemonics for the notes of the scale, and ask them to make up their own (see photograph on page 33).
  Every **G**ood **B**oy **D**eserves **F**avour - represents the notes on the lines of the stave.
  F A C E - represents the notes in the spaces of the stave.

SOL-FA (Singing Names)
Teach the children the singing names of musical notes -
    Do Re Mi Fa So La Te Do (this is the Sol-Fa scale)
    low   high

The Sol-fa system uses these names for all the notes in the scale, rather than written symbols, until the children can hear and understand sounds - in a similar way to children not being taught to read until they can talk.
The starting note - Do - can be any note at all, and the distance (intervals) between each note remains the same.

- Write the Sol-fa scale vertically on the board, and practise singing up and down it with the children. Play games with them, such as singing with their eyes closed, singing the next note up from one you give them, etc. (The Curwen hand signs developed by Curwen and adapted by Kodaly could be introduced at this stage.)

- Use the magnet board or finger puppets. Place one magnet/puppet higher than the other, and tell the children that one is called So and the other is called Mi. Ask them to discover which is which (So is the higher one, as So is a higher note than Mi).

- Sing up the scale slowly, asking the children to stop when you get to Mi. Draw a horizontal line next to it (the Mi line). Repeat for So (the So line). The children can use these two lines, which are the beginning of a traditional five line stave, to write tunes on So and Mi. Sing these tunes using the Sol-fa names, and play them on tuned instruments.

- When the children have had lots of practice singing, playing and writing tunes using So and Mi, introduce La. Sing songs such as 'Rain, rain, go away', 'Ring a ring o' Roses', 'It's raining, it's pouring' and 'I'm the King of the Castle', all of which use So, Mi and La. Ask the children to identify So and Mi, and they will find that there is a new note - La.

It's raining, it's pouring
Mi So Mi La So Mi

The old man is snoring
Mi So Mi La So Mi

He went to bed and bumped his head
Mi So So Mi La So   So Mi

And couldn't get up in the morning
Mi   So   So So Mi Mi La So Mi

Sing these songs using the Sol-fa names and hand signals to show the pitch of each note.

● Go back to the diagram showing the two line stave. Add La to it, telling the children that there is no need to draw a new line for it as it is next to So, and can go in the space above the line.
The children can now write tunes to sing and play, using So, Mi and La.
They should now be able to write their music using the two line stave and also Sol-fa notation.

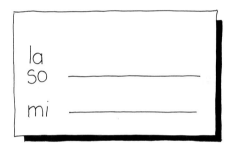

● Make a series of cards showing three note tunes which the children can use to practise singing and playing.

● Ask them to make cards showing tunes for their names.

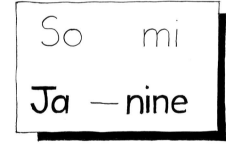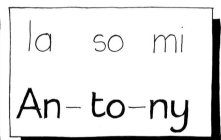

● Introduce the rest of the scale very slowly, providing plenty of reinforcement at each stage. The order in which they are usually introduced is:
So Mi La Do(low) Re Do(high) Te Fa

● Write your own simple songs to reinforce the notes as they are introduced, e.g.

He-llo chil-dren, How are you?
s   s   m   l   s   s   d

● Sing them using both the words and the Sol-fa names.

Singing

As a classroom activity, singing can fulfil many purposes. One preconception which is hard to dispel is that the teacher needs to be able to sing well in order to teach songs to children. Young children are extremely uncritical of their teacher, and their enjoyment of singing precludes any ideas they may have about their teacher's singing voice. Enjoyment is the main aim of singing with young children. The main things a teacher needs are confidence, a sense of pitch and rhythm, and a sense of fun! This will be infectious and will result in productive, stimulating singing sessions. Songs can act as an excellent starting point for creative work (see photograph on facing page).

Singing can be used to stimulate or to calm down a group. It has the effect of bringing everyone together and creates a sense of sharing and participation. There are often children in the class who have difficulty in joining in with other group activities, but who can share in collaborative singing. No complex equipment is needed, and therefore a singing session can be spontaneous, offering a welcome break from the demands of an academic day.

Just give it a try - you will be heartened by the enthusiastic response you will get. One way to start is to 'Sing the register'. Call the children's names out in a tuneful way, and ask them to sing their reply back to you.

CHOOSING SONGS
The first thing to consider is the subject of the song.
   Will it appeal to the group?
   Is it relevant to other learning going on in the classroom?
   Could it stimulate imaginative and creative activities?
   Is it a teaching aid, e.g. does it help the children to learn the days of the week?
   Does it have a good tune?
   Will they be able to understand the words and concepts? (Words can be substituted if too difficult.)
   Does it have an easy-to-learn chorus where everyone can join in?
   Is it within the children's singing range, i.e. not too high or too low? (Children's voices tend to be lower than we think.)

Build up the children's repertoire of songs to include:

   action songs
   singing games
   quiet, thoughtful songs
   humorous songs
   informative songs
   traditional rhymes and songs

If a song proves too hard to master, abandon it!

WARMING UP ACTIVITIES
● Start off with some general warming up activities which are enjoyable, set the scene and also allow you to find your feet gradually.
● Ask the children to sit up straight and comfortably with their hands in their laps. Ask them to imagine that they are puppets with strings attached to the tops of their heads, to remind them to keep their heads up and their backs straight.

Paintings in response to favourite songs

- Ask the children to take a deep breath with their hands on the base of their rib cage, to feel the stomach and bottom ribs move out. Practise controlling the outward movement of the breath, so that it is not let out all at once. Breathe in to a count of six, and then let it out to a count of six. Try it when singing 'lie' on the outward breath. Increase the number of counts.
- Choose a vowel sound - ay, ee, eye, o, oo - and sustain it on a middle range note, one that is comfortable for you and the children. Stop, and repeat with another vowel sound. Then try starting with one and changing it into another without stopping.
- Now make the same vowel sound, but this time make a beautiful, high sound, 'as high as the clouds in the sky'. Don't let them scream! Try this for a sound 'as low as the worms in the earth'.
- Repeat this for loud and soft sounds. Ask the children for ways to make the sound - 'Make a high, loud aaaaah' etc.
- Who can make the longest sound? Use this opportunity to relate the amount of air escaping to the volume and length of the sound.
- Now experiment with short sounds. How many can the children think of?
- Sing 'lalalala' as quickly as possible. Really make the tip of the tongue work hard. Note how all parts of the mouth have to work harder to make short crisp sounds such as 'papapapa'.
- Try putting together a sequence of short and long sounds.
- Extend this by reintroducing the concepts of high and low, and loud and soft. The children should be able to produce a huge variety of short sequences. Ask them to demonstrate and then try to copy each other.

TEACHING A SONG

- Talk to the children about the song - its subject, any new or strange words, whether it has a chorus, etc.
- If you can, play it to them (for example, on a piano or guitar), and ask what kind of music it is - happy, sad, spooky, etc. If the opportunity arises, it is a good idea to have played the tune of a new song at times such as when the children are coming into assembly, to familiarise them with the music before being formally introduced to it.
- Say the words of the songs to the rhythm of the music and get the children to repeat them, line by line.
- Sing a short section, with the children echoing. Then sing longer sections in the same manner. Make sure each section is learned accurately. If there are problems with the tune, sing it to 'la' or hum it. If a particular word or phrase proves difficult, practise that in isolation. Vary this by getting the children to sing it to you in groups, or quietly/loudly/happily, etc. Do this for as long as the children's attention span lasts - you may have to return to it the following day.
- Sing the whole song through together.
- Do not add instrumental or body percussion accompaniment too soon, as the distraction of instruments will be too much when a song is not known really well.

IDEAS TO ADD VARIETY TO SINGING

- Ask the children to sing in different styles, for example,
  'Sing with wide open eyes'
  'Sing with a smile in your eyes'
  'Sing with your eyebrows high up'
  'Sing with a dance in your voice'
- Hum songs. (To hum, the lips should be relaxed, the teeth a little apart and the lips just touching. The children should feel the vibration in their noses.)
- Play games such as 'Stop and Go' when a pretend traffic sign is held up and the children sing aloud on 'Go' and in their heads on 'Stop'.
- Sing very quietly so that the only person you can hear singing is yourself.
- Sing as loudly as you can, without shouting.
- Sing as if your voice is coming out of the top of your head.
- Ask the children to sing in groups (for example, according to their hair colour, or shoe colour etc.).

STARTING A SONG

The children need to be clear when, and on which note, to start singing.

- Sound the first note on a pitch pipe, tuned instrument, or with your voice if you have a good sense of pitch. Hum 'la' for the starting note and get the children to echo you.

- Ask the children to come in together using a variety of methods, which could include:
  - Body language: breathing in with an expectant look on your face, hands raising, etc.
  - Counting in: sing on the starting note 'l,2,3,and' for songs in 4 time, or 'l,2,and' for songs in 3 time.

- Do not be hesitant when starting the children in a song - they will lack confidence and will not get going until halfway through it! Find which method you feel happy with, and stay with it.

Movement

It is a red planet and it was strange. There were strange kinds of birds there, and a caterpillar which spurted out water. It had craters which spurted out sort of magic smoke. If you touched this smoke you would become a fairy. The sun was square and gave out blue and pink rays. It was a very magic place and I would like to go back there.

Natty.

The jelly on the planet is all different colours. The flowers are different. They have got red bits that hold them up and red bits inside. It made me feel like I wasn't going back to earth ever again. I had this lovely creature that when I touched it it gave me lovely dreams. It was purple. About the flowers, they had orange leaves on them, and one of them was yellow. It was a special one.

Alfie

YI danced on a new planet!

My planet is the red one in the corner. My picture is about the journey to get to the planet. And its got jelly and rabbits have drawn the rainbow in the picture. I have got stars and diamonds in space too.   Judd

It was very soggy and it was very strange and I picked up a little flower, and I felt that it was very squelchy. I saw a strange sort of animal, and it smiled at me and it wanted to make friends. There was strange sort of clouds and there was an oval moon. There are flower diamonds on the bushes here. I liked it there and I didn't want to come home.

Loes

Creative work arising from dance activities

Through games and activities, children can be helped to a deeper understanding of music. The emphasis should be on fun and enjoyment, with a sense of achievement. Children should wear suitable clothing and have bare feet, providing that the floor surface allows this. The children should be encouraged to move in a way that expresses their response to the music through their whole body language.

- Some children find it consistently difficult to move to a beat. Take the hands of two children who experience this difficulty, and walk between them, helping them to feel the pulse.
- Play games such as 'The Farmer's in his Den', 'Lucy Locket', 'In and Out the Dusty Bluebells' and 'Tideo'. Children love the familiarity of repetition, which allows a constant reinforcement of skills such as inner hearing and experience of rhythm and pulse.

USE OF SPACE
The group needs to be able to make use of the available space, and to be able to move around others freely but with control. Ideas can be developed, such as:

- Distribute hoops or posts around the room, so that the children move in and out of them to encourage good spacing.

- Musical Statues can be played, where any children who are near enough to touch each other when the music stops have to sit down.
  These skills need to be constantly practised, as do the skills of making a line or a circle, and getting into groups.
- The children also need to know how to react promptly to a set of instructions, possibly the same ones as those used in P.E. lessons. They should be able to stop at both positive signals (e.g. a sound such as a bang on a tambourine, or the word 'stop!') and negative ones (when the stimulus, e.g. music, ceases).
- All children should be given the chance to be leaders and demonstrators, with encouragement given to the less secure and confident in the group, by perhaps suggesting that he/she demonstrates his/her work with a partner, or is the leader of a small group of friends.
- Instructions given by the teacher should be clear and precise, and should make use of verbal stimuli by altering the tone and speed of the voice, i.e. 'Move slowly and heavily' would be spoken in a deep and strong voice.
- Ask children to demonstrate when their actions are particularly good.

STIMULI
As with other creative activities, the stimulus can come from a range of directions:
  The weather or seasons; a class outing; a visitor to the school; a current topic; puppets; music from a variety of sources and cultures; animals, birds or insects; transport; a story or poem; machinery.

TYPES OF MOVEMENT
A basic selection of movements could include:
  walking, running, skipping, galloping, side-stepping, joining hands, linking arms, clapping (own hands, partner's hands, own knees, partner's knees).

NURSERY RHYMES
Once the children have a repertoire of nursery rhymes that they can sing confidently, make up simple dances to them, with movements such as:
  In pairs, face your partner
  Take two steps backwards
  Take two steps forwards
  Link arms and skip round in a circle
  Take two steps to the side,   etc.

DALCROZE
Emile-Jacques Dalcroze was a Swiss composer and educator who developed a teaching method known as Eurythmics, the aim of which is to help children to understand music 'from the inside' rather than just hearing it as a sound outside themselves.

Stamp the Music
Stand in one large circle, facing inwards. Sing a song, or listen to a piece of music, and establish the beat by clapping. Replace the clapping with stamping on the spot.

Walking the Music
- This skill needs lots of patient practice, but is an invaluable way of feeling and responding to the music. It requires lots of repetition, but with imagination, to avoid boredom. It consists of walking the beat of a piece of music.
  - Sit the children in a circle, and sing a well known song, such as Frère Jacques.
  - Sing again, and clap the beat at a steady walking speed.
  - Do it again, using a different body percussion, e.g. tapping the floor.
  - Ask the children to go and stand in a space. Sing and clap the song again.

- Then ask the children to walk the beat of the song while singing it. Some may find it difficult, and will initially walk the rhythm - the words of the song. Go back to clapping the beat and remind them that the beat is like a steady heartbeat throughout the song. Then try to walk it again. It may help to get everyone walking at the same speed, and then begin the song once the beat has been established.
- Split the class into two and let one group walk the beat while the other stands and sings the song. Swap over.
- Keep the class in two groups. Let the groups take it in turns to sing and walk the song, taking a line each, alternately.
- Working individually again, ask them to sing the song, while walking the first line, standing and clapping the second, walking the third, etc.
- Finally, try walking the beat of the song, while clapping the rhythm, and vice versa.
- Repeat the above, using another song or a piece of recorded music.

Running the Music
- Sit the children in a circle again and set up one half of the group clapping a steady, fairly slow beat. Lead the other half into clapping twice as fast, i.e. two claps for every one by the other group. This would be 'running speed'. Swap over.
- Reinforce this by using other body percussion.
- Repeat the activity of clapping at walking speed while singing the song.
- Sing the song again, but clap at running speed.
- Ask half the group to clap the walking beat, and the rest to clap the running beat, while singing the song. Swap over.
- Ask the children to go and stand in a space. Stand and clap the running beat while singing the song. Then try to run the beat while singing - taking little steps on tiptoe.
- Reinforce as for the walk.

Slow Walking the Music
- The above can be repeated, using the 'slow walk', or stride. The children will find this one easier if they take giant steps. The slow walk is twice as slow as the walk. Therefore, when half the group is clapping the walk, the rest would only clap on every other beat.
- Try games such as 'Slow walk to the count of 4, Walk to the count of 4, Run to the count of 4, Stand to the count of 4'.
- While singing a well known song, or listening to music, ask half the group to step to the walking beat and the other half to step to the running beat, after clapping the relevant speeds first.

Notation
- Cards introducing musical notes can be introduced during the above activities.
    The 'slow walk' would be represented by a minim.
    The 'walk' would be represented by a crotchet.
    The 'run' would be represented by 2 quavers.

- The French names for musical notes could also be introduced:
    minim   taa-aaa
    crotchet   taa
    quavers   ta-te

● Once the children are adept at walking the beats of songs and other music, they can be told at which speed they should be moving, through the use of cards held up by helpers.

Rhythm Games

● Divide the group into four, and send one group to each of the four corners of the room. Ask them to move in a clockwise direction to the next corner in a manner you specify, e.g. 'quickly and quietly', and stop there. Repeat. Change the style of movement each time, and the direction occasionally. Incorporate the notation cards (as above) into this game.
● Repeat the above, but use musical stimuli. Any instruments can be used, and again the speed and volume should be varied. The variation in the stimuli should be very marked at first, e.g. a slow and steady drum beat, followed by a rapid, delicate triangle trill. Repeat using notation cards.
● Ask the group to walk, skip, gallop or run. Stop them and immediately ask them to clap what they were doing with their feet.
● Reverse the above, asking them all to clap a rhythm with you, e.g. a skipping rhythm, and then, on your signal, ask them to translate that rhythm into movement.

Step your Name

● Remind the children about how to clap their names. Now ask them to 'walk' their name, taking a step for each syllable.
● Sit in a circle. Set up a slow beat, tapping the floor to keep the pulse steady. Go around the circle with each child whispering his name in turn, the first syllable on the beat, for example,

Jake	Jake	Jake	Jake
Lau - ra	Lau - ra	Lau - ra	Lau - ra
Da - ni - el	Da - ni - el	Da - ni - el	Da - ni - el

● Next, ask the children to whisper their names all at the same time, perhaps six times.
● Ask them to go and stand in a space. Play the pulse on the drum this time, and ask the children to whisper their names again, as before. Then ask them to walk their name as well as say it. Finally, stop the chanting and just step in silence.

Dance your Name

● Following work on clapping the syllables in their names, get the children to work out a simple choreography to go with their name, for example

KA	-	THER	-	INE
arms round in a circle		hands on hips		jump in air

Ka - the - rine

● Ask the children to get into small groups to join their choreographies together into a 'Dance of Names'.

Clapping Numbers

Sitting in a circle, set up a chant of 1...2...3...4, whispering the numbers. Call out 'ONE' and everyone claps when they say 'one'. Once this is established, shout 'TWO' and instead of clapping on the number 1, everyone now claps on 2. then call out 'THREE' and 'FOUR'. Extend this by calling out two numbers at once, e.g. 'ONE and FOUR'.

Expanding Claps

Sit in a circle, and count in the following pattern:

1...12...123...1234...12345...123456...1234567...12345678...123456789...

Ask the children to chant this with you, and to clap every time they say the word 'one'. Get them to describe a circle with their hands in between the claps, so that their hands are back together in time for the next clap. Ask the children what happens to the size of the circles they make. Extend this by counting up to nine, and then decreasing back to one.

Four to One

On the piano, choose two notes that sound harmonious together, one for the right hand and one for the left hand. With the left hand, play a note and hold it for the count of four. With the right hand, at the same time, play a note on each of the four counts, i.e.

left	1				1				1			
right	1	2	3	4	1	2	3	4	1	2	3	4

Divide the group into two. Ask one half to move around the room to the left hand notes, and the other half to move to the right hand notes.

Twinkle Twinkle

Lay out hoops on the floor around the hall, well spaced out. Sit down and sing 'Twinkle, Twinkle, little star'. Ask the children to clap on the last beat of every line:

Twin-kle twin-kle li-ttle STAR
How I won-der what you ARE

Once that is established, ask the children to walk around the room, not in the hoops, still clapping on the final beat. Finally, instead of clapping, they can walk around, and jump into a hoop on the last beat of every line - it doesn't matter if someone else jumps in the same hoop, but they can't use the same hoop twice. They will find that they have to plan their movements ahead, in order to be able to jump into a hoop at the right moment.

A similar game can be made up using the song 'Polly Put the Kettle On', when Suki comes to visit Polly inside a hoop.

Ball Play

Using the same theme of time and space as 'Twinkle Twinkle', there are lots of games that can be played using soft balls.

● Ask the children to find partners and to sit facing each other, one with a ball. Chant together, 'l...2...3...4' SLOWLY! On the count of 'One', the ball is rolled to the other person, who rolls it back on the next 'One'.

● As the children become more adept, ask them to roll the ball on 'One' and try to judge the distance and speed, so that their partner receives it on the count of 'Four'.

● Try it to other counting patterns, e.g. l...2...3.

● Play the same games in a circle, rolling to people across the circle.

● The children can also play with balls individually, e.g.

1	2	3	4
bounce	catch	bounce	catch

● Let them devise their own routines to counting, e.g.

With a partner, to the count of 4 - 1...each throws their own ball in the air
2...each catches their own ball
3...they roll their ball to their partner
4...they pick up the ball that was rolled to them

● Try to do the above games to music - making sure it is slow music at first! Before the children move, make sure that the beat has been established first by clapping and counting aloud.

Hand Jives
● Introduce the children to the concept of 'hand jiving', where the hands dance to music. Use any actions that you already know, or invent your own and ask the children for their ideas. Do it first in a circle, and practise the movements.
● Then build up a routine, with the whole group doing the same actions altogether, while counting, for example,

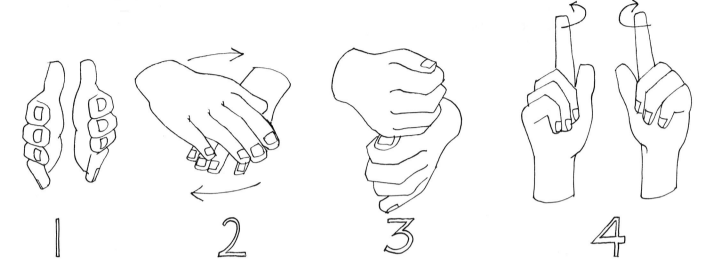

● Ask the children to sit in their own space, or with a friend, and devise their own hand jive to the count of 1...2...3...4... When finished, let them demonstrate, reminding them to count out loud when doing the actions.
● Ask half the class to sing a song which is in four time (i.e. has four beats to the bar, and to which you can count 1...2...3...4), and ask the rest of the class to do their hand jives to the song. Swap over.
● Try the hand jives to pre-recorded music with a heavy beat. Before the children do the actions, sit and clap the beat, counting out loud '1...2...3...4' to establish the beat for them. Don't choose a piece of music that is too fast!
● Repeat the same activities, but with clapping patterns. Ask the children to demonstrate the latest 'partner clapping' songs, and then ask them to make up their own. How imaginative can they be before they are not able to keep up with the music?
● Try and make up a circle clapping pattern when the entire group stands in one large circle and performs a series of pre-arranged movements while counting aloud (or silently). This is very satisfying, but takes patience and practice. Suggestions could include:
   Tapping the shoulders of the people on either side of you
   Patting your knees
   Patting the knees of the people on either side of you
   Spinning around on the spot
   Clapping your hands together
   Crossing knees and hands
   Jumping up in the air,   etc.

Four at a Time
● Choose a very rhythmic piece of music, e.g. rock and roll. Sit in a circle, and clap/tap/slap to establish the beat. Find the heavy beat, and count 1...2...3...4 (it is very likely to be in 4 time). Stop the music, but continue the counting. Make a movement, for example, put your hand in the air on the first beat, i.e. every time you count 'one'.
● Now try it on the count of 'two', 'three' and 'four'.

● Introduce another movement, e.g. hands on head, and try the first movement on 'one' and the second on 'two'. Continue until you have decided on a movement for each of the four beats, for example,

1	2	3	4
hands in air	hands on head	clap hands	slap knees

Practise this until it is fluent, with all the group doing the same actions. Then ask the children to go and stand in a space. Keep counting aloud until the children are really confident, and then try it counting silently. Get the children to close their eyes for a while, and then reopen them and see if they have kept together.
● Now reintroduce the music and see if they can do it at speed!
● Try it as a round, with half the class starting first, and the rest starting on the count of 'three'. Don't forget to tell them how many times to do it.
● Repeat the above activities, but let the children devise routines where they can move across the floor, for example,

1	2	3	4
step	**bend knees**	**jump**	**turn around**

Double circle games
Arrange the children in a double circle, i.e. one circle inside another. Make up games such as:
- The two circles walk around either to the beat or the rhythm. They could move in opposite directions.
- The inner circle walks round to the beat, while the outer one walks in the opposite direction to the rhythm.
- On a given signal, the circles change direction, or change roles, i.e. change from walking the beat to walking the rhythm.
- One circle could walk to the music, and the other could run, or slow walk.

Block Marching
Arrange the children in tight formation, e.g. five rows with four children in each row. Make sure they are touching shoulders, and as close as is comfortable to the row in front. Use this grouping pattern to walk the beat of music or songs. The children will have to solve problems such as turning corners or changing direction.

DANCE
There is a natural relationship between music and dance, and young children often move instinctively to music. By moving to it, they can be helped towards a deeper and more sympathetic response to music.

When choosing music to use, be clear of what the children are to experience or learn from it. Use material from a wide range of cultures and traditions.

When thinking of composing a dance, introduce the recording to the children on several occasions beforehand. Use it as a piece of listening music in the classroom, and as a stimulus for other creative work. As the children begin to understand the music, they will be able to provide more suggestions to use in dance (see photograph on page 41). The best way to find movements that go with a particular piece of music is to move to it and see how the body responds. Take guidance from elements in the music such as beat, rhythm, melody, words (if a song), speed, dynamics and texture.

Listening Skills

Listening is a skill which needs to be taught if effective learning is to take place in any situation. There is so much extraneous sound in the world today that children often hear but don't listen. There is a need for them to be able to shut sounds out, but some do not have the discrimination to be able to know when it is necessary to listen.

Auditory skills are needed for basic literacy, and through musical activities, these skills can be developed in an enjoyable and productive way. It is important that the games and activities are carried out in silence, to encourage careful listening.

Children need to be able to follow verbal instructions, take messages, express feelings and inform others.

● Try the following activity with the children, to demonstrate 'selective listening'. Ask someone to read into a tape recorder for about one minute. Try to do this where there is a certain amount of background noise. Play this back to the children and ask them to re-tell you the story they have just heard. There should not be any problem with that. Then ask them about anything else they heard (background noises). It is unlikely that they noticed or could identify any.

● Discuss the need for communication through sounds - to communicate danger, to express pleasure and happiness, to attract a mate, to gather the young, to guard territory, to show pain, fear or hunger, and to offer comfort, etc.

● Go on a listening walk, to listen to sounds both inside and outside the school building. Record these sounds (see photograph on facing page).

● Have quiet listening times at different times of the day. Discuss the nature of the sounds heard, and also their quality. Use this to introduce new vocabulary to describe sounds. Classify the sounds into categories, e.g. high/low, nice/nasty, near/far, loud/soft, short/long. Another way to classify could be origin of sound, either human, animal or mechanical.

● Play Chinese Whispers.

● Clap a nursery rhyme and ask the children to identify it.

● Have a range of objects made from different materials, e.g. metal, plastic, rubber and a range of surfaces, e.g. wood, fabric, concrete. Take turns in dropping the objects on the different surfaces, and talk about the resulting noises.

● Sort a selection of instruments into types of sounds they make, e.g. loud/short, gentle/rough. This quality of sound is known as *timbre*.

● Fill a selection of pots with substances. Guess what is inside them. Explore the sounds made by different substances in identical pots, and identical substances in different pots. Make two pots of each substance, and ask the children to find the pairs, by shaking them.

Which pots go together?

Pictures inspired by familiar sounds around the school

Play Blind Man's Bluff
When a child is caught, he/she must say a poem, and the blindfolded child must try to identify the person by the sound of the voice.

Key Word Stories
Pre-arrange with the children a range of 'key words' to listen for in a story which you will tell them. When they hear any of these key words, they must make a pre-arranged sound or movement, e.g. whenever you say 'pig' they must snort, touch their noses or wiggle their eyebrows, depending on what was decided by the group.

Commands
Using a piano as a percussion instrument (i.e. use it only to make sounds - you don't have to be able to play a tune on it), tell the children to do as the piano tells them, for example 'When the piano plays a high note, come towards it. When it plays a low note, go away from it.' This can also be played in a circle - 'When the piano plays quietly, creep in to the centre of the circle. When it plays loudly, creep outwards again.' Keep an eye on the children - once they are all crowded in the centre, don't keep playing quietly!

Simon Says
Play a version of the game when the leader claps, or plays an instrument, rather than speaks 'Simon Says'. The group only follows the instruction when the correct clap is given or the correct instrument is played.

Coded Dance
Pre-arrange with the children movements connected with instruments, for example, a tambourine rattle means 'run', and a steady drum beat means 'march'. Build up a sequence of movements, following the sounds made by a group playing the instruments.

Hidden Instruments

Allow two children to choose an instrument each. Discuss with the group the name of each instrument, the sound it makes, and how to play it. Ask the children to hide (e.g. behind a simple screen) and decidebetween them who should play first. The rest of the class try to guess which is playing. The child who is correct takes the place of the player.

There are lots of variations on this game:
- Increase the number of hidden instruments gradually.
- Allow two to play together.
- Do not show the hidden instruments to the group before the game starts.
- Get a child to play a steady drum beat all the time while the hidden instrument is playing. The group then has to discriminate between the drum and the unknown instrument.
- Allow two instruments to play together, and then one drops out. The group has to guess which it is that has dropped out. Increase to three, etc.
- As the children's auditory discrimination improves, choose instruments which make similar sounds, e.g. jingle bells and tambourine.
- Use voices or body percussion sounds.

Goodbye Messages

When dismissing the children, give each group a different sound as their cue to go. This sound could be a body percussion sound, e.g. tongue click, a clapping pattern, a note on a tuned instrument, or a sound on a percussion instrument. Get the children to close their eyes, and stand to leave when they hear their sound. 'Tricks' are very popular in this game - giving the last remaining group the wrong message!

The Orchestra Game

This is a musical version of the Shopping Game. In a circle, everyone has a turn at building up the orchestra - 'I was in the orchestra and I went BANG!' 'I was in the orchestra and I went BANG! and swishhhh'...Try this with the children making body percussion sounds rather than spoken sounds.

Copy Me

Sit in a circle with a set of two or three instruments in the centre. One child goes into the centre of the circle and plays a short sequence on the instruments. He/she then chooses a friend to go into the middle and echo the sequence.

Heads and Shoulders

Choose two children and give each an instrument. Ask one to hide and the other to stand where everyone can see him/her. The latter child plays a constant rhythm on the instrument, whereas the unseen one plays sporadically. When they hear the hidden instrument play, the children put their hands on their heads. When it stops, they put their hands on their shoulders.

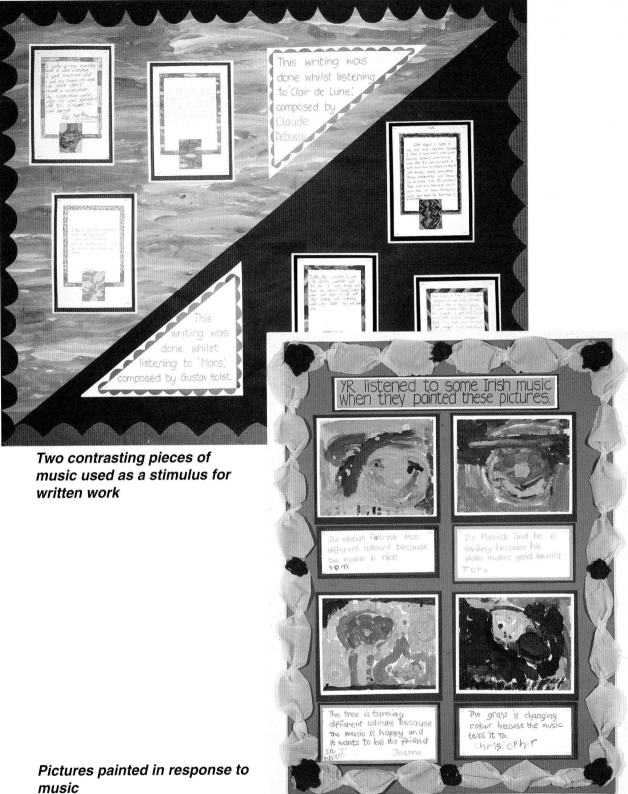

Two contrasting pieces of music used as a stimulus for written work

Pictures painted in response to music

LISTENING TO MUSIC

Listening to music with children has several purposes and can lead to different conclusions:
- for pleasure, when the listening itself is the end product
- to develop musical understanding
- to stimulate other creative activities (see photograph above).

Children need to be helped to learn how to listen actively, to discuss and then to listen again. They should be exposed to as wide a range of musical styles and ideas as possible.

Study the music first, before listening with the children, in order to be able to help them listen for some of the following:

Beat   Clap or tap the beat.
Is it fast or slow?
Is it weak or strong?
How are the beats grouped? Listen for the heavy beats, which are counted as one, and count steadily. It may be -

           1212 = a march or polka
           123123 = a waltz
           12341234 = rock and roll
           123456123456 = a skipping rhythm, as in 'Boys and Girls come out to play'.

Rhythm   Is it a regular or irregular rhythm?
Does it change throughout the piece, or does it stay the same?

Melody   Is the tune gentle and flowing, or does it jump around?
Is there one main tune, or a short one that is repeated in different ways?

Dynamics   Does the volume stay the same, or are there loud and soft sections?
If so, why are they there (to add tension, to calm, to frighten, etc.)?

Texture   Is there one instrument playing alone, or is there a group of them?
Is the tune being played by a soloist, with other instruments providing a backing? (Jazz often uses this technique.)
Is there a mass of rhythms all intertwining? (African drumming or gamelan)
Are all the instruments playing together to make one big tune? (as in a Symphony Orchestra)

Structure   Are there themes in the music that are repeated later?
Are there contrasting parts, e.g. loud next to soft, fast next to slow?
Music is often written using one of the following forms:

           Binary - A (first tune) B (second tune)
           Tertiary - A B A (as in 'Hot Cross Buns' or 'Twinkle Twinkle')
           Canon - like a round with the sections coming in one after the other
           Rondo - ABACAD, as in a song with a chorus between each verse

English

Telling a story which uses rhythm and body percussion

THE VOICE
- The spoken language is itself a form of music-making. Investigate the effects of changing pitch (high and low) and rhythm (fast and slow) when speaking, and also of altered meaning when different words are emphasised in a sentence:
  '**Was** that you?'   'Was **that** you?'   'Was that **you**?'

- With the children sitting in a circle, experiment with saying their names in different ways - loud/soft, fast/slow, high/low, smoothly/jumpily, etc.

- Choose a simple phrase, e.g. 'Baked beans on toast please'. Ask the children to take it in turns to say the phrase in different ways, for example, to sound frightening, worried, scared, polite etc. The rest of the group could guess what feeling the speaker is trying to convey.

- Take a theme, such as 'Summer Holidays'. Ask each child to suggest a phrase, and choose a style in which to deliver it, which they feel matches the meaning of the phrase, for example:
  Swimming (said in an excited, enthusiastic voice)
  Fishing (said in a relaxed, quiet voice)
  Playing on the computer (said in a mechanical voice) etc.
  Remind the children to consider the effects of dynamics, volume, accent and pitch.

- Sing a well known song, but substitute vocal sounds for key words, for example,
  'She'll be comin' round the *whistle* **when she comes'**
  Increase the complexity by substituting more than one word per line, for example,
  She'll be *pop!* **round the** *whistle* **when she comes'**
- Ask the children to record themselves reading a short passage, and see if the other children can identify them. Then repeat this activity, but encourage them to disguise their voices this time. Ways to do this may include:
  - a handkerchief over the mouth
  - holding the nose
  - tapping the Adam's apple gently while talking.

SOUND EFFECTS
This is one of the simplest and most enjoyable ways to get children to create musical accompaniments to the written word. Begin by reading or telling a story to the children, and then encourage them to devise relevant vocal accompaniments.

- Tell the story of The Lion Hunt, with the children making the appropriate actions and sounds. This is an 'echo' piece, where the children copy whatever you say, in time to 'patshing', which is slapping the knees alternately, to a steady beat. Set up the patshing first, and then begin, making up the words as you go along, and adapting them to suit the situation and the children involved. The important thing is to speak rhythmically, in time to the knee slapping.

patshing	LEFT RIGHT L R		L R L R
teacher	*We're going on a lion hunt*	**children**	*We're going on a lion hunt*
patshing	L R L R		L R L R
teacher	*What a lov-ely day*	**children**	What a lov-ely day
patshing	L R L R		L R L R
teacher	*Don't forget your gun!*	**children**	*Don't forget your gun!*

The story continues in this style: going round, through, over and under lots of obstacles such as bridges and muddy fields (using vocal and body percussion sound effects), until the cave is reached. Go in on tiptoe (fingertips patshing) in the dark, very scared - 'I can feel something furry!' Scream and run out, back through the obstacles, and home again. (See photograph on page 53.)

- Ask the children to write stories which deliberately include the theme of 'Up and Down', e.g. the adventures of someone who lives on the top floor of a block of flats. Ask them to devise sound effects for their stories, using tuned percussion instruments such as metallophones.

Joe climbed up the ladder.   He picked an apple.   Then he dropped it into the basket.

- Record a range of different kinds of film music, e.g. exciting, scary, creepy, happy. Discuss with the children how each piece of music makes them feel. They could write stories from these excerpts.

- Watch a silent movie, with the purpose of listening to the musical accompaniment.

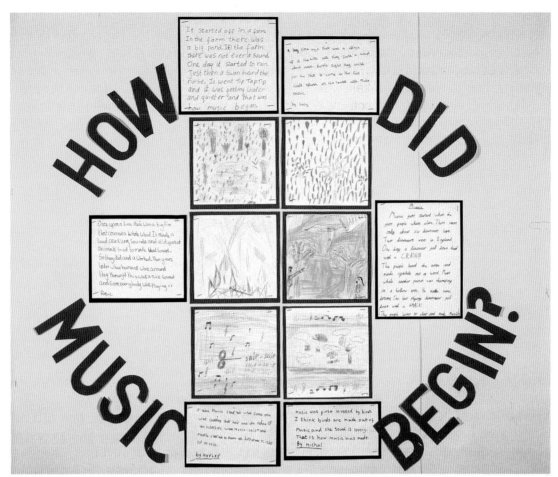

Imaginative stories about the beginning of music. Discuss the beginnings of music, emphasising that this activity is imaginative, and that the children can be as creative as they wish

● Poems or stories to which they can compose 'scores' could either be written by the children, or come from other sources, including poems written specifically for this activity by the teacher. Make sure that there is a wide range of 'noise makers' available to the children, and encourage them to search the classroom and their homes for objects which make a sound. Some ideas may include:
  - the plastic cases inside chocolate boxes (autumn leaves crunching under foot)
  - a wet cork rubbed on a glass bottle (a bird singing)
  - two water-filled bottles for blowing across (a cuckoo)
  - a metal tray being hit or shaken (thunder)
  - a mug being lowered upside down under water, and then lifted out (pop!)
  - small stones being rubbed together (walking on a pebbly beach).

● The children need to devise methods of writing down their accompaniments so that others can come and play them. They can also be tape recorded with a reading of the poem, and the other children could try and guess how the sounds were made.
● The children could write puppet plays incorporating their sound effects.
● There are many published stories, some of which are listed in the Bibliography in this book, which lend themselves to having sound effects added.
● Challenge the children to find ways of making a specific sound effect such as a squeaky door.
● Record a series of sound effects, e.g. footsteps, a door opening, a whistle, etc., and use this as a stimulus for story or poetry writing by the children.
● Record a selection of television theme tunes and talk to the children about how they feel when they hear a particular theme tune, e.g. 'I get angry because when that programme comes on, I have to go to bed.'

SPOKEN LANGUAGE

● Many rhythm games are based on spoken language, and can be used to enrich the children's vocabulary. For example, during a topic about Food, names of foods can be chanted, together with appropriate rhythmic percussion accompaniment, and made into 'Sound and Speech Poetry':

(whispered)　　　**Ba-na-nas grapes and che-rry pie**
same rhythm repeated very quietly on tambourine
(quietly spoken)　　**Ba-na-nas grapes and che-rry pie**
same rhythm repeated quietly on woodblock
(chanted)　　　　**I said Ba-na-nas grapes and che-rry pie**
same rhythm repeated on drum
(shouted)　　　　　**All taste good to me!**
shake on the tambourine, finish with two drum beats.

● As part of a topic on Weather, the children could create a piece based on chants and accompanying instruments and movement. In three groups:

Group 1	**Group 2**	**Group 3**
(chant 4 times and pat the beat on knees)	(chant 4 times with tambourine trills)	(chant 4 times with maracas)
Rai-ny day, rai-ny day	**Hail-stones, hail-stones**	**Wind blow-ing, wind blow-ing**

● An idea such as this could be developed by bringing all the groups together, one at a time, and building up to a crescendo (loud climax) perhaps with a thunder roll, and then fading away, one group at a time, to silence. In an activity such as this, the spoken word is being used like a musical instrument, with the words and the way in which they are spoken, together with their accompaniment, creating an atmosphere.

WRITING IDEAS

● Listen to music by the children's favourite performers. Discuss with the children their ideas about the lifestyle of pop stars. Ask them to write short mock 'interviews' with the performers of their choice. These could be recorded, or made into a play.

● Rewrite the words, or add verses, to suitable songs such as 'When I was One', 'Aiken Drum' or 'If you're happy and you know it'.

● Using a 'cumulative' song, such as 'There was an Old Lady Who Swallowed a Fly' or 'There's a Hole in my Bucket, dear Liza', put a series of drawings and/or text in story sequence.

● Play games based on the sounds of words, e.g. alliteration or calligrams.

● Explore poems written using nonsense language, such as Edward Lear's 'In the Ning Nang Nong', where part of the attraction of the poem is in the sounds of the words. Ask the children to write their own nonsense poems, encouraging them to enjoy the sounds of new words.

● Read *lunch* by Denise Fleming (the Bodley Head), which is a book containing the noises made by creatures. The children could write their own versions.

● *Carnival of the Animals and Other Poems* by Mick Gowar (Viking/Penguin) is a collection of poems written to accompany the musical suite 'Carnival of the Animals' by Camille Saint-Saëns. The poems can be used in conjunction with listening to the music, as a stimulus for creative work such as poetry-writing or illustrations.

● Make up 'sound words' and illustrate them, e.g. '**SSHHLLERRREEEEE**' is the sound our dog makes when he skids across the floor.'

● Write poems called 'What is loud? What is soft?' -
    'As soft as a bee's kiss on an evening sunflower,
    As loud as the smoke alarm at toast-burning time.'

● Using a fable, such as those written by Aesop, ask the children to compose a short song for one of the characters, and to make a tune for their song.

● Tell the children about the lives of famous composers and use this as a stimulus for writing, such as diaries, letters, newspaper articles, etc.

● Repeat the above with the stories of scientists who worked in the area of sound, for example Alexander Graham Bell and Thomas Eddison.

● **Spelling** can be helped by practising words with an emphasis on rhythm:
    - Spell the word aloud to devise its rhythm pattern: clap it, move to it, and play it lots of times, for example -   b-e-c-a-u-s-e   t-o-m-o-r-r-o-w
    - Make up little chants - t-h-e spells 'the'
                        t-h-e- spells 'the'
                        Yes it does, you know it does,
                        t-h-e- spells 'the'!

READING
● Make large song books, illustrated by the children, which they can read together.

● Use cards with key words written on them, which can be held up at the appropriate point when a song is being sung.

● Play 'Pairs' or 'Bingo' with cards of key words from songs. Ask the children to name the song that the word is from before they can pick up their pair.

● Using cards with the titles of songs the children know, cut them up and ask the children to reassemble them to find the name of the song.

Science

Music is organised sound, and sound is caused by vibration of a material. Sound is an energy, a movement you detect with your ears and which is interpreted by your brain.

● Encourage the children to FEEL vibration:
  - Put their figures on their throats while speaking
  - Rest their hands on the speaker of a radio or tape recorder
  - Blow through tissue wrapped around a comb
  - Feel a cat's body when it is purring
  - Feel the string of a guitar when it is sounding
  - Set off a tuning fork and touch their cheeks with it
  - Hold a blown up balloon in front of a speaker playing music and feel the air inside the balloon vibrating.

● Encourage the children to SEE vibration:
  - Sprinkle sand or rice on the skin of a drum and then hit it and watch the sand jump
  - Hold a ruler down over the edge of a table and flick it
  - Set off a tuning fork and immediately dip it into a bowl of water
  - Twang an elastic band and watch the movements
  - Stretch a piece of balloon over the end of a toilet roll. Glue a piece of silver foil on the balloon, and shine a torch on to it so that the light reflects onto a wall. Speak into the tube and watch the spot of light on the wall. The voice makes the air in the tube vibrate, and the balloon skin vibrates in turn.

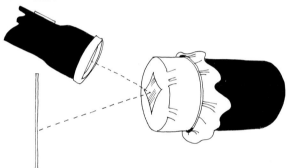

● Suspend a table tennis ball next to a loudly sounding triangle. Watch what happens.

● Encourage the children to HEAR vibration:
  Repeat the above experiments, but vary the intensity of the movement to compare the volume of the sound to the size of the vibration, i.e. the more gently the elastic band is twanged, the smaller the vibration and the quieter the resulting sound.

● Study instruments to discover how the sound is made (see photograph on facing page).

HOW SOUND TRAVELS
Very simply, air is made up of millions of particles of gases. When a drum is hit, it vibrates and causes the gas particles next to it to vibrate too. The particles next to those vibrate in turn, and so on, as in the 'domino effect'. Use a Slinky or marbles to demonstrate.

● Sound vibrations travel through air at approximately one mile every five seconds. Send a child down to the far end of the playground to do some hammering, or burst a balloon. Ask the children to watch, and see what they notice.

● During a storm, show the children how they can count between the thunder and lightning to calculate how far away the storm is (every five seconds represents a mile).

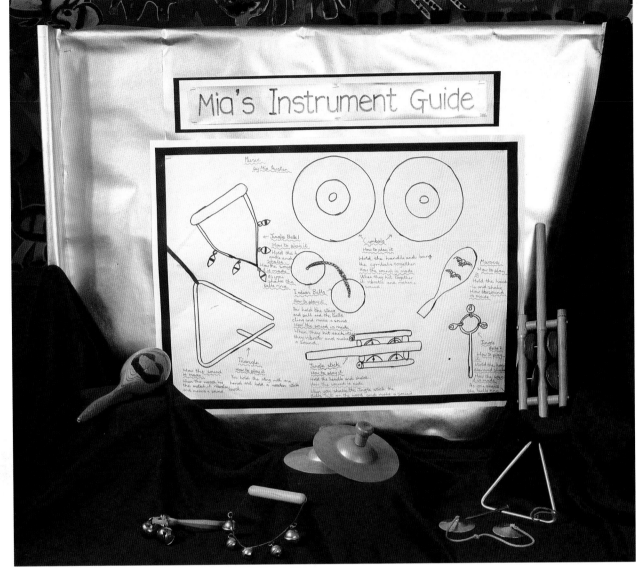

Drawings and explanations of how sounds are made on instruments

- Get the children to devise tests to check each other's hearing.
- Ask them to investigate whether sound travels through other materials as well as through air.

SOUND PROOFING AND ENHANCEMENT OF SOUND
- Discuss noise pollution and situations where sound proofing could be necessary.
- Talk about the need for care of our ears. Ears can be damaged by loud sound from any source, including personal stereos.
- Ask the children to investigate the effectiveness of various materials in sound proofing:
  Use a ticking clock or a radio: put it in a box and ask the children to suggest and devise tests for a range of materials to wrap around it to deaden the sound.
- Make ear muffs and investigate the effectiveness of various materials for sound proofing.
- Talk about times when sound needs to be amplified.
- Ask the children to devise ways in which human hearing could be enhanced. (Be sensitive to children's feelings about their ears.)
- Make simple ear trumpets and megaphones. Investigate their effectiveness over distance. Are larger ones more effective?

- Make stethoscopes. Does the length/thickness of the tube matter? Does the size of the funnels matter?

● Study pictures of animals and discuss the ways in which they are able to hear more acutely as one of their survival or hunting techniques (see photograph on facing page).

● Get the children to try to pinpoint the origin of a sound when blindfolded. Does it help to turn the head? Investigate the effect of blocking up one ear.

● Sound can bounce off hard surfaces. This is known as sound reflection, and is an 'echo'. Ask the children to find some places in the school which are good for echoes, and some that are bad for echoes. If possible, visit a recording studio or modern concert hall, to look at the ways in which sound can be controlled. This control of the quality of sound through use of materials and shape is known as 'acoustics'.

● Investigate a reflecting sound.
Use a ticking clock, and place it at the end of a long tube. Position the other end of the tube near the wall, and put another tube at an angle to it. Listen at the end of this tube, moving it until you can clearly hear the ticking as the sound bounces off the wall and travels down the tube.

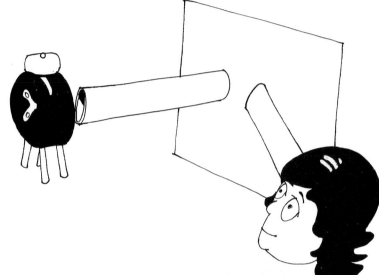

● Talk about SONAR which is used by ships to navigate and to find underwater objects.
SO = sound   NA = navigation   R = range
Bats use a similar technique.

PITCH
Music is made up of sounds of many pitches, from very high to very low. The rate of vibration per second is called 'hertz', and the lowest sound audible to the human ear is about 16 hertz. The pitch of a note is determined by its speed of vibration - the faster the vibration, the higher the note. As a general rule, the more there is to vibrate, the slower the vibration.

● Using the ruler over the edge of a table, get the children to investigate the relationship between the length of the section of ruler that is being twanged and the speed of the vibration. They should find that the longer the ruler is, the slower the vibration, and the deeper the resulting sound.

● Use a guitar. Put your finger firmly on one string at the top, pluck the string hard, and then immediately slide your finger up the string, pressing down firmly. The note gets higher as the string gets shorter.

● Arrange chime bars in order of size. The longer the bar, the slower the vibration and the deeper the sound.

● Make up a water xylophone. (See photograph of water chimes, page 7.)

Studying the ways that animals hear

● Use a waxed paper drinking straw to make a pipe. Blow hard to get a note, and then snip off the end of the pipe as you blow, and the note will get higher. As the pipe shortens, there is less air inside to vibrate, and therefore it vibrates at a faster speed.

Flatten end, then cut to a point.

● Speed of vibration can also be affected by adjusting the tension of the strings on a stringed instrument or the skin of a drum - the more tension, the faster the vibrations and the higher the sound.

TIMBRE
The timbre of a sound is its quality. The taste of a lemon is quite different from that of a strawberry, and the sound of a cymbal is quite different from that of a woodblock.

● Set up a display showing a variety of examples of one particular type of material, e.g. paper or metal. Provide a wide range of examples such as tissue, cards, kitchen/greaseproof paper, watercolour paper, blotting paper, tracing paper, newspaper, corrugated card, etc.

● Play a 'Hidden Materials' game, where a child is behind a screen with a range of different materials. He/she makes a sound with one of them, and the others try to guess which material it was. Materials could include sandpaper, wood, rubber, ceramics, glass, metal, etc.

● Investigate the noise made by dropping a coin from the same height, on to a variety of different surfaces. Make a list of the surfaces in order of loudness.

Maths

MEASURING
● During work on length, investigate the relationship between the length of bars on chime bars or xylophones, and their pitch.

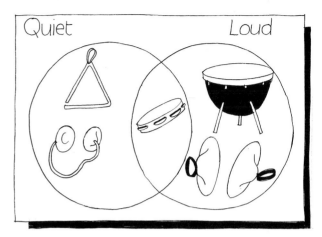

DATA HANDLING
● Compile lists of objects that make loud sounds, and objects that make quiet sounds. Make a chart to show the information - are there any characteristics that the objects in each set have in common, for example, are all the 'loud' objects made of metal?

● Carry out surveys, such as 'Favourite Pop Stars', 'Favourite School Songs', or 'Sounds I really don't like'. Draw up graphs to display the information (see photograph on facing page).

COUNTING SKILLS
● Sing counting songs and rhymes, such as 'Ten Green Bottles'. Get the children to compose their own, at their level of mathematical skills, e.g. counting in twos.

● Play clapping games, counting the claps.

● When standard notation has been introduced, the children can investigate the relationship between 'running notes' (quavers), 'walking notes' (crotchets) and 'striding notes' (minims) - i.e., easy fractions.

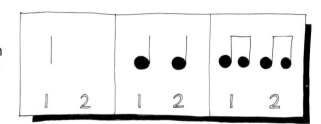

● Play Huggy Bear. Play a rhythm on a tambourine - sometimes skipping, sometimes running, etc. and ask the children to move around the room accordingly. At a given signal - a trill or bang on the tambourine - the children stop, and you call out 'Huggy Bear two!' and they will quickly move into groups of two, and put their arms around each other. For 'Huggy Bear three' they form groups of three, etc. (To lessen any potential awkwardness for children left over, either intervene and be a 'Huggy Bear' yourself to complete a group, or start another rhythm on the tambourine quickly.) Investigate with the children the results of dividing the class into groups, for example, 'How many groups of four can we make? Are there any children left over? How many?'

Recording favourite songs

ALGEBRA
Use pattern making as a form of notation for instrumental work. Repeating patterns can lead to work on rhythm, e.g.

$$* \quad * \quad * \quad \# \quad \# \quad * \quad * \quad * \quad \# \quad \# \quad * \quad * \quad * \quad \# \quad \#$$

(* could be a triangle, and # could be claves.)

● Addition patterns can also be used. The addition sums composed when asked to 'find a way to make 5':

4 + 1 = 5	could be 4 beats on a drum and I on the maracas
2 + 3 = 5	could be 2 beats on a drum and 3 on the maracas
5 + 0 = 5	could be 5 beats on a drum and 0 on the maracas

WEAVING PATTERNS
● Study the patterns in woven fabrics, and then ask the children to weave their own 'fabric', using coloured strips of paper. The resulting patterns can be 'played' using the same number of instruments as colours used in the weaving.

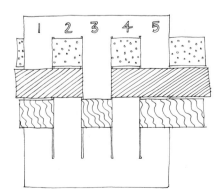

Humanities and R.E.

GEOGRAPHY
● Learn folk dances and folk songs from other countries. If possible, arrange visitors or dance groups to come to demonstrate and teach the children.

● Go on a 'voyage' round the world, introducing the music of all the countries you visit on the way - link with photographs, maps, slides, books, artefacts etc.

● Look in an atlas to find the birthplaces of famous composers.

● Use patterns in the local environment as inspiration for graphic notation scores (see chapter on Art). For example, get the children to do closely observed drawings of an old wooden door, or a paved pathway.

● Design and construct a simple Sound Path in the school grounds. Mark out a pathway, and use various materials to cover the path which make a sound when walked on.

● Carry out surveys around the school and in the grounds, to discover the kinds of sounds heard in different areas.

● Find examples of musical instruments which have their origins in the type of environment in which they are used, e.g. Alpen Horns, designed to carry sounds across mountain ranges; African Drums to send messages; or, Steel Drums made from the oil drums left at ports.

● Listen to the folk music of different countries.

● Use legends, folk tales and story-telling styles of other countries as a stimulus for making up songs and using rhythm, e.g. the Willow Pattern story. Invite storytellers in to school, in particular those from countries such as Jamaica, who use dance and rhythm as part of their story-telling.

● Make up raps, which originate from the story-telling styles of the West Indies.

HISTORY
● Ask the children to research the songs and rhymes sung by their parents and grandparents when they were at school. Make recordings of them and learn them, together with playground games that may go with them.

● Discuss the reasons for singing and making music, which have remained the same for centuries:
       to celebrate - wedding, home-comings, etc
       to worship - pacifying or praising gods
       to help work - to keep in rhythm (marching, hauling ropes, etc.)
       to protest - Blues, songs from the days of slavery, songs from the Sixties, etc.
       to socialise - story-telling, moral training.

● Learn 'call and response' songs such as 'Day-O' or 'Hill'n'Gully Rider' from the days of slavery.

● Dance and its associated music is a stimulating way to present History. Contact the English Folk Dance and Song Society.

Using artefacts from other cultures as an inspiration

Prehistoric music: Study cave paintings. Ask the children to do drawings in this style showing ways of making music, e.g. blowing in shells, drumming on hollow trees, plucking the string of a bow, etc.

Egyptian music: Study tomb paintings of music-making and singing, and photographs of musical artefacts (The British Museum has a good range of these). Ask the children to write poems to put to music, e.g. a song sung by a farmer asking the Nile to flood, or by slaves building a pyramid.

Old Testament: Tell the story of Joshua and the walls of Jericho. Get the children to write it as if it were the main story of a newspaper of the time.

Ancient Greeks: Talk about the role of the gods in Ancient Greece, and about the 'muses' (hence the word 'music') who gave inspiration to composers. Re-tell or act the stories of Pan, Orpheus and Ulysses.
Adapt a story, e.g. The Three Little Pigs, into the style of the Greek Theatre, with a singing chorus.

Romans: Write marching songs, or songs to praise a victorious soldier.

Medieval:	Listen to song recordings of 'Plainsong', e.g. Gregorian chants. Find out about the life of the monks who made the music of this time.
Middle Ages:	Write a story in cartoon form, about the adventures of a minstrel on his travels.
Renaissance:	Learn a dance of this period, e.g. a Pavanne.
Baroque/ Classical:	Find out about the lives of composers of this time. Set these stories in the context of life and events at that time.
Romantic:	Talk about the way in which composers of this time were free from confines of having patrons, and dealt more with emotions and feelings in music. Listen to a selection of recordings and talk about how they make the children feel. Do drawings and paintings to show these feelings.
Modern:	Listen to a range of 'popular' music, to include Jazz, Blues, Reggae, Rock and Roll, and Rap - all these are traceable to African roots.

● Examine through photographs or artefacts the way in which instruments have changed and developed through history.

RELIGIOUS EDUCATION

Music is used as a way of celebrating, praising and communicating feelings in all cultures. It is an expression of social attitudes on such things as love, death, honour, misery, prayer, celebration, loyalty and protest.

● Listen to music from a range of religions, played to celebrate weddings, e.g. 'Hava Negila' (Come and Be Happy) in the Jewish tradition, or to brighten the darkness of winter, or to celebrate birthdays of great teachers, as in the Gurupurb festivals in the Sikh religion.

● Watch a film of a Carnival, or listen to calypso and steel band music. Carnivals originated as celebrations before the commencement of Lent, with all its associated denials ('carnival' comes from the Latin words 'carne vale' which means 'farewell to flesh').

● Learn songs about the environment, and emotions such as anger, joy or sadness, caring for others, people who help us, etc. Use the songs as starting points for discussion.

● Write 'thoughtful' songs with the children.

● Music is one common factor among all peoples, for which one needs no spoken language. Get the children to experiment with improvising music on instruments to express human emotions. Play guessing games about which emotion is being portrayed.

● Discuss how the coming of commercial entertainment, for example television, may have affected the life style of people, in the way that families rarely play instruments or sing together to make their own entertainment any more. Talk about times when the children may have experienced family parties, e.g. Christmas, and how it felt to them to be actively involved in this.

Art

A visual portrayal of word sounds

Patterns from Music
Select pieces of suitable music for the children to listen to. Provide them with drawing materials - if planning to produce 'rough' drawings first, use a quick medium, e.g. oil pastels. Make sure that each child has plenty of paper. Talk to them first about what you expect from them, encouraging them to close their eyes and let the music suggest patterns and colours. Try to steer clear of 'images', such as battleships or gardens, encouraging abstract shapes and patterns, as suggested to them by the music.

Who makes music?
Discuss the types of people who make music, and make a collage of the children's own pictures mixed with photographs of music-making.

How does Music make you feel?
Get together a small selection of different types of 'atmosphere' music, e.g. Saint-Saëns' 'Danse Macabre' ('Dance of Death'), Scott Joplin's ragtime music, Beethoven's 6th Symphony ('Pastoral') etc. Provide the children with face shapes cut out of paper, and ask them to draw faces to show how they felt when they heard each of the pieces of music.

Shaky Chain

Make a long chain from strong string to stretch across the classroom, with a series of objects hanging from it that make a noise when shaken. Provide cords hanging down for the children to pull (gently!) to 'play' the chain.

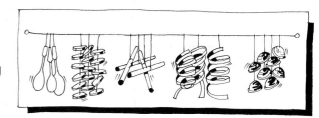

Noise Machine

Make a class three-dimensional collage of a 'Noise Machine' (or dinosaur, a vehicle, etc.) which can be played with beaters.

Mobiles

Use different types of materials to make sound mobiles. Encourage the children to categorise the materials into 'tinkling', 'rattling', 'knocking', etc. Materials may include: tinkling - balls of silver foil, milk bottle tops, nails, washers, chains; rattling - segments from plastic egg boxes, nut shells, pasta, shells; knocking - cardboard tubes, cotton reels, small blocks of wood.

Instruments

Percussion and tuned instruments are excellent objects for closely observed drawings done in either pencils, watercolour or inks.

Design a cover

Study a range of CD, cassette and record packages. Ask the children to design covers either for music they have all listened to, or for their favourite artists, or for a title given to them, e.g. 'Moments of Summer'.

Illustrate a song

Let the children choose one of the songs they sing at school, and draw a picture of what they think it is about (see photograph on page 63).

Word Sounds

Discuss onomatopoeia (words whose sounds reflect the meanings). Ask the children to represent the sound visually (see photograph page 67).

Musical Images

As an extension to work on graphic notation, discuss with the children what sounds a selection of abstract images could suggest.

Study some carefully chosen piece of abstract art with the children. Choose a pathway to travel across the picture from one side to the other. Trace the path with your finger, and ask for suggestions from the children as to how the colour or shape being crossed at that moment may be translated into sounds. For example:

Starts on blank area	Silence
Heavy line	one loud drum beat
Little dots	many quick beats on a woodblock
Heavy line	one loud drum beat
7 Vertical lines	Glissando on metallophone seven times
Spots	Cymbal played with finger tips, fading away

Perform the music with a child acting as conductor, tracing the pathway across the picture. As the children begin to understand this concept, ask them to paint abstract paintings with areas of both flat colour and pattern. Use these to stimulate composition, as on page 67.

Glossary

Accent	a stressed word or note to make it louder than the rest
Bar	a unit of time in music, containing a certain number of beats
Beat	the steady pulse through a piece of music, that you may want to clap to
Body percussion	sounds made using different parts of the body
Canon	music where more than one voice or instrument plays the same theme, but at different times
Classical	music composed roughly between 1750 and 1830 - orderly music, giving emphasis to clarity, beauty and balance - having a permanent value
Concerto	a work in which a solo instrument (or instruments) blends and contrasts with an orchestra
Dynamics	the contrasts between loud and soft in a piece of music
Glissando	a scale played up and down an instrument very quickly
Harmony	two or more notes playing together and sounding pleasant
Improvisation	making up music spontaneously
Interval	the gap between two notes
Melody	the 'tune' - a line of notes going up and down, with a rhythm
Ostinato	a pattern of notes, movement, speech or rhythm, being repeated over and over as an accompaniment
Note	an individual musical sound
Pentatonic	a five note scale, where the distance between each note is the same
Pitch	the highness or lowness of a sound
Pulse	another word for *beat*
Rhythm	the pattern of notes, being long and short
Scale	a set of notes ranged in order of pitch
Score	the written form of music
Sonata	three or four pieces of music called movements, put together
Stave	a set of five lines for musical notation
Symphony	a set of pieces or movements written for an orchestra
Timbre	the tone of a sound, e.g. mellow, thin, scratchy, etc. that makes it possible to identify individual voices or instruments
Tuned instrument	an instrument on which a melody can be played
Untuned instrument	an instrument which can play only one note or sound

Resources

Books to read in conjunction with listening to music
Peter and the Wolf, James Riordan, (OUP).
Famous Children, series of books (Gollancz Children's Paperbacks).
Nini at Carnival, Errol Lloyd (Picture Puffin).
Faber and Faber produce a range of easy piano books which tell the stories, together with extracts of the score. Titles include: *Swan Lake, Nutracker, Mikado, Magic Flute* and *Hansel and Gretel*.

Books for Children
To compose accompaniments or sound effects to:
Beware, Beware, by Susan Hill (Walker Books)
A Scary Story, by Peter Bailey (Scholastic)
Stormy Weather, by Amanda Harvey (Macmillan)
One Stormy Night, by Ruth Brown (Andersen Press)
Stormy Day and Sunny Day, by Clair Henley (Dent)
Beeswax the Bad's Noisy Night, by Andrew and Paula Martin (Picture Corgi)
Crocodile Bear, by Gail Jorgensen and Patricia Mullins (Red Fox)
Peace at Last, by Jill Murphy (Macmillan)
The Musical Life of Gustav Mole (Child's Play International)
Little Beaver and the Echo, by Amy Macdonald and Sarah Fox-Davies (Walker Books)
Goodnight Owl, by Pat Hutchins (Little Greats)
lunch, by Denise Fleming (The Bodley Head)
We're Going on a Bear hunt, by Michael Rosen (Walker Books)
I'm Going on a Dragon Hunt, by Maurice Jones (Picture Puffin)

Books for Teachers
Scholastic Practical Guides - Music, by Barry Barker
Oxford Primary Music 1, by Jean Gilbert & Leonora Davies (OUP)
The Beaters Series by Schott & Co:
    Strike 5, by Peter Sidaway
    Dr Knickerbocker, by Diana Thomson & Shirley Winfield
    Music in Action, by Michael Lane   (Schott & Co.)
Music for Fun, Music for Learning, Lois Birkenshaw (Holt, Rinehart & Winston)
High Low Dolly Pepper, Veronica Clark (A&C Black)
50 Nursery Songs - for use with Kodaly teaching (Boosey & Hawkes)
The Kodaly Way to Music, by Cecilia Vajda (Boosey & Hawkes)
Let's Make Music Music for All: 1, Prill and Martin Hinckley (Novello Music Projects)
Music All the Time, A Music Course, by Wendy Bird and Elizabeth Bennett (Chester Music)
Musical Starting Points with Young Children, by Jean Gilbert (Ward Lock Educational)

Cassettes
'Fun With Music', series of cassettes by EMI, telling stories using the music of famous composers.
Titles include 'Romeo and Juliet', 'Mr Handel's Firework Party', 'Sleeping Beauty' and 'Swan Lake'.